John Paul II – Witness to Truth

# John Paul II – Witness to Truth

Proceedings from the Twenty-Third Annual Convention
of The Fellowship of Catholic Scholars,
September 22–24, 2000, in Atlanta, Georgia

Edited by Kenneth D. Whitehead

ST. AUGUSTINE'S PRESS
South Bend, Indiana
2001

Manufactured in the United States of America.

1  2  3  4  5  6   07  06  05  04  03  02  01

**Library of Congress Cataloging in Publication Data**
Fellowship of Catholic Scholars. Convention (23rd : 2000 :
Atlanta, Ga.)
   John Paul II, witness to truth : proceedings from the
   Twenty-third Annual Convention of the Fellowship
   of Catholic Scholars September 22–24, 2000 Atlanta,
   Georgia / Kenneth D. Whitehead, editor.
      p.  cm.
   Includes bibliographical references.
   ISBN 1-58731-395-2 (alk. paper)
   1. John Paul II, Pope, 1920 – Congresses  I. John Paul
   II, Pope, 1920– II. Whitehead, K. D.
BX1378.5 F44 2000
282'.092 – dc21                          2001003840

∞ *The paper used in this publication meets the minimum requirements*
*of the American National Standard for Information Sciences –*
*Permanence of Paper for Printed Materials, ANSI Z39.48-1984.*

# CONTENTS

# INTRODUCTION

Those who have attended the annual conventions of the Fellowship of Catholic Scholars know that these conventions are organized around a chosen theme, and that the invited speakers, usually scholars of some prominence – who may or may not be members of the Fellowship – then deliver talks dealing with one or another aspect of the chosen theme. Usually the speakers are academic specialists in the topics they present. Following the convention itself, it has been the custom to collect the addresses delivered in the course of the convention into a volume of "Proceedings" that can serve as a permanent record, which is then distributed to the entire membership of the Fellowship (since no more than about a fifth of the membership attends any given convention).

This volume, *John Paul II – Witness to Truth,* brings together between two covers the addresses delivered at the Twenty-third Annual FCS Convention held in Atlanta, Georgia on September 22–24, 2000. As the title indicates, the chosen theme this year was the achievement of Pope John Paul II – or, rather, more exactly, only *some* of the *many* achievements of the extraordinary man who has occupied the Chair of Peter since October, 1978 (the same year the Fellowship itself was founded).

When the FCS Board of Directors decided to focus on the pontificate of Pope John Paul II as the chosen theme for this year's convention, it quickly became apparent that the usual Friday-through-Sunday-morning format of FCS conventions would allow treatment only of selected parts of the immense achievement of the present pontiff. Nevertheless, under the able program chairmanship of Msgr. William B. Smith, speakers of both outstanding knowledge and unusual distinction were found and agreed to address key aspects of the Wojtyla pontificate. Readers of the following pages will accordingly be amply rewarded with a greatly enhanced understanding of the thoughts and actions of Pope John Paul II – as the participants at the convention itself were (there was wide agreement that this was one of the best FCS conventions ever!). Moreover, readers will find these pieces unusually readable; two of them were actually transcribed from tapes as delivered, and the other speakers quite successfully connected with their audience while following their written texts.

It was especially gratifying to have George Weigel as the keynoter for the convention, following closely upon the publication of his outstanding biography of John Paul II, *Witness to Hope*. Each of the speakers, though, succeeded in illuminating some particular aspect or aspects of the pope's immense overall achievement, and, with these contributions reprinted here, this volume hopes to serve as an important contribution to the understanding of the remarkable pontificate of many achievements that we have been witnessing over the past more than two decades in the history of the Church of Christ.

# PROGRAM CHAIRMAN'S INTRODUCTION

## Rev. Msgr. William B. Smith

Welcome to Atlanta, welcome to all – in *this* city, it is "Y'all"! Still, welcome to our convention of the Fellowship of Catholic Scholars!

Within a calendar year, Atlanta has been host to a World's Series, a Superbowl, and the All-Star Game. Now comes the Fellowship of Catholic Scholars. To any clear-thinking person, i.e., all disinherited Democrats, there is a clear progression of importance and prestige in this Atlanta sequence!

True, there is less media coverage for us, which is okay. Also, your salaries are much deflated from those of the athletes who preceded you. But recall the advice of St. Thomas More to Richard Rich: "Richard, be a teacher!" "Be a teacher" – which many of you are. St. Thomas More was not impressed with Rich's pursuit of the post of Attorney General of Wales. My advice is the same: "Be a teacher"! We don't need another Attorney General Reno!

Since it is the Jubilee Year, 2000 – in part, a year of big apologies – let me first apologize to you for not having invited Garry Wills to come and read some passages from his new book, *Papal Sin* (New York: Doubleday, 2000). I was even hoping we might be able to get John Shelby Spong as a respondent to read balancing passages from his book, *Here I Stand* (San Francisco: Harper, 2000). But all that really would be a "structure of deceit," since both of these men only write about what they used to believe in.

Our only real topic is largely one person: Pope John Paul II, and his Witness to Truth. Come October 16th, John Paul II will have been pope for 22 years; he was elected on that date in 1978. It may be an accident of time, but the Fellowship of Catholic Scholars was founded in that same year, 1978. An accident of time. A coincidence. I have a friend who defines "coincidence" as "those times when God chooses to remain anonymous." Maybe so. Maybe not.

Our keynote speaker, George Weigel, closes his remarkable biography of John Paul II by citing G.K. Chesterton's characterization of St. Thomas More, namely, that he was, above all, "historic." By this is meant that he represented at once a type, a turning point, and – ultimate destiny. If there had not been this particular man at that particular moment, world history would have been different. By extension, if there had not been this particular pope and this particular pontificate, to close the last century and to open this one, the present history of the Church would have been different. Perhaps very different.

Thus, I welcome you all to this convention. Let me thank in advance all the generous presenters who will speak to and about some of the many aspects of this remarkable pope, John Paul II; and to and about some of his remarkable contributions as a genuine, indeed, a remarkable Witness to Truth.

Thank you for coming. I do hope that you will enjoy and profit from the presentations as well as from the good fellowship at the convention. This meeting may not be "historic," but our subject is certainly historic. My hope is that you will enjoy both the scholarship and the fellowship at this Catholic gathering!

As they say in the upper echelons of the Vatican: *Habe suavem diem! Have a nice day! Plus aut minor ( more or less)!*

Rev. Msgr. William B. Smith, S.T.D., is a moral theologian and dean at the archdiocesan St. Joseph's Seminary at Dunwoodie, Yonkers, New York. He is nationally known as an expert on pro-life and bioethical questions and is a frequent speaker and contributor to symposia on these topics. He conducts the regular monthly "Questions Answered" column on moral theology in the *Homiletic & Pastoral Review*. He is a past president of the Fellowship of Catholic Scholars and a recipient of its Cardinal Wright Award.

# KEYNOTE ADDRESS
## JOHN PAUL II – WITNESS TO HOPE

### George Weigel

Thank you very much, Monsignor Smith, and thank you, my old and dear friend Gerry Bradley, for the invitation to share this evening, and at least a part of your convention, with you tonight. During the three and a half years that I was preparing my book *Witness to Hope*, I had the distinct impression that I was being supported by a great ocean of prayer. I think many of you in this room were part of that, and so I would like to take the opportunity to thank all of you who supported *Witness to Hope* spiritually, as well as the many of you who supported it and me intellectually.

On May 19th of this year, which is to say, one day after the Holy Father's eightieth birthday, Vittorio Messori, an Italian journalist whom many of you will remember as the pope's interlocutor in *Crossing the Threshold of Hope*, published an astonishing op-ed piece in the Italian daily, *La Stampa*, in which he made the argument that 22 years of "Slavic exceptionalism," as he put it, were enough; and that there was, in his view, a wide consensus within the leadership of the Church on the necessity of a return to what he called "Italian normality" in the papacy. Now, while this strikes me as something vaguely akin to someone confidently predicting a year ago that Orrin Hatch had a lock on the Republican presidential nomination, it was, I think, an interesting straw in the wind. It indicated how poorly Messori – who is, I think we have to say, a very well-situated observer – how poorly he had grasped the range of the accomplishment of John Paul II, an accomplishment which,

among many other things, means that the next conclave
will be very, very different from its predecessors.

But I wonder if we, too, aren't occasionally susceptible
to the Messori syndrome. Have we really measured accurately the great achievements of the past 22 years? Caught
up, as so many of us are, in what can seem an endless
stream of controversies, we too may be tempted to focus so
closely on what *hasn't* happened in this pontificate that we
may fail to grasp adequately what *has* happened – and
what that means for the future.

So permit me this evening to suggest that there are nine
enduring achievements of great consequence in the pontificate of John Paul II, achievements that have decisively
reconfigured the Catholic world for the 21st century.

The *first* of these achievements is, I believe, that John
Paul II has recast the papacy for the 21st century and
beyond by retrieving the biblical concept of the office of
Peter in the Church, that is to say, he has returned the papacy to its evangelical roots. This has had a tremendous
impact not simply on the Church, but on the world.

About three months ago a friend of mine – a distinguished political commentator, Jewish in background –
said to me out of the blue over dinner one night: "Who's
going to be the next pope?" I said: "I haven't got the faintest
idea." He said: "Well, will he be like John Paul II?" And I
said: "Yes." I thought that the model of the publicly
engaged pope, a great witness to the dignity of the human
person on a global scale, had been so set in place by this
pontificate that it would be difficult to imagine a return to
the papacy as an office in which minding the shop was the
primary task. My friend said: "That's good," and then he
laughed. I said: "What's so funny?" And he said: "You
know, in 1978, I couldn't have cared less who the next pope
was going to be, but now I care a lot. Now it means something to me."

This is a very telling comment, it seems to me. The
Church and the world now expect the pope to be an evan-
gelist, a pastor, and a witness to, and defender of basic

human rights, as well as a global moral reference point. That was not the case 22 years ago. But it is very much the case today; and that, it seems to me, is the first great and enduring accomplishment of this pontificate.

But I wish to add immediately that this is not simply the accomplishment of a singular personality, but rather the accomplishment of a pope who is self-consciously the heir of the legacy of the Second Vatican Council. And this, I would suggest, is the *second* great achievement of this pontificate, namely, that it has secured the legacy of Vatican II in its fullness as the Council which was intended to revitalize the Church as an evangelical movement in order to address *the* great crisis of our time: the crisis of the idea of the human person.

Those of you who have had a chance to read the book know that this was Karol Wojtyla's understanding of Vatican II from a time even before the Council formally convened. As some of you remember, I'm sure, in 1960, the ante-preparatory commission – the preparatory commission before the preparatory commission – sent a letter to all of the bishops of the world saying that the pope has had this strange idea that we should get all of you guys together, so what do you think we should talk about? 2400 bishops wrote in; those of you who have worked with the documentation on the Second Vatican Council know that those responses fill eight linear feet of shelf space, in huge folio volumes! If you read through those materials, you will find that they are quite striking for a number of reasons. But perhaps the most striking thing is that the great majority of the submissions from bishops around the world had to do with internal, ecclesiastical housekeeping items: bishops who wanted to be able to give permission for X, Y, and Z without referring it to Rome; who wanted certain changes in Canon law, and so on.

My favorite submission came from the archbishop of Washington, Archbishop Patrick A. O'Boyle, whom many of you knew, I'm sure. Archbishop O'Boyle's letter had six or seven of these housekeeping items in it, and then he had an eighth suggestion. He said the Council should pronounce, in light of the doctrines of creation and redemption, on the possibility of intelligent life on other planets! When I read this in the archives of Rome I just cracked up, and the archivist said, "What's so funny?" And I said, "Well, I should have thought that the archbishop of Washington would be more interested in the possibility of intelligent life in his own diocese than on other planets!" – a situation which has not changed in the last 40 years.

But amidst all of this concern over internal bric-a-brac, if you will, there came into the ante-preparatory commission a very different kind of submission, a letter from a then 40-year-old auxiliary bishop in Krakow, Karol Wojtyla. He did not send in an agenda of internal housekeeping items; he sent in a philosophical essay – an essay on the crisis of humanity in the sixth decade of the 20th century. Why, he asked, had a century which had begun with such great expectations of a maturing humanity, growing into a new solidarity, why had this century produced, within 50 years, two world wars, 3 totalitarianisms, oceans of blood, mountains of corpses, and the greatest persecution of the Church in history?

His answer, quite simply, was that all of the sorrow of the 20th century derived, in one way or another, from defective *humanisms*, that is, from defective concepts of the human person, human origins, human community, and human destiny. And Wojtyla proposed that the great task of the Council was to rescue the humanistic project by reconstituting, or revitalizing, as I said a moment ago, the Church as an evangelical movement in history, thus returning the great humanistic project to its true trajectory, which aimed, he argued, straight into the Holy Trinity Itself.

Now, with this background, this concept of what the Council was for – so different from the Xavier Rynne notion of the Council as cowboys and Indians, good guys and bad guys, and "whose-in-charge-here?" arguments! – with this concept of the Council, then, there is a great Spirit-led effort to gather the Church together for the rescue of the human-

istic project in its moment of great peril. It is no surprise
that the two most frequently cited texts from the Council in
this pontificate have been *Gaudium et Spes* #22 and *Gaudium
et Spes* #24. In *Gaudium et Spes* #22, you will remember, the
Council fathers tell us that Jesus Christ reveals both the face
of God and the true meaning of human existence. In
*Gaudium et Spes* #24, the Council fathers teach that the
meaning of our lives is to be found in self-giving, not in self
assertion. Put those two ideas together and I think you
have Wojtyla's optic on the Second Vatican Council.

The law of the gift, as I call it in the book, written into
the human heart, from the beginning, is an expression of
the self-giving love that constitutes the interior life of God
– Father, Son, and Holy Spirit. To live that law of the gift in
history is to enter, in an anticipatory way, into the communion with God for which humanity was intended from
the beginning.

Here Vatican II and John Paul II are saying to the
deeply confused world of late modernity: here is a destiny
greater than you can imagine, and it is yours because you
are greater than you think you are. Thus the Pope has laid
out the theological and philosophical foundations for what
I think is of particular interest to a group such as this – the
foundations for a great revival of Christian humanism in
the 21st century, a revival whose necessity, whose urgency,
is as apparent as every morning's headlines.

This Christian humanism has inspired *two* of the other
great public achievements of this pontificate (which are the
*third* and *fourth* of the nine enduring achievements of John
Paul II which I mentioned at the beginning); they are: the
pivotal role John Paul II played in the collapse of European
Communism; and the detailed outline of the free and vir-
tuous society which John Paul II has laid out over the past
decade.

By demonstrating, during the decade-long preparation
for the revolution of 1989, that culture is the most dynamic
force in history, and that Christian faith can be an agent of
human liberation in history, John Paul II also reminded free

societies, old and new, that democracy and the free economy are not machines that can run by themselves. Rather,
both free politics and free economics must be tempered
with and disciplined by a vibrant public moral culture.

By positioning the public Church as an agent of cultur-
al transformation, John Paul II completed the transition of
Catholicism to what can be accurately described as a post-
Constantinian period in its history. I believe this process
began with the pontificate of Blessed Pius IX and has
reached its definitive moment in the pontificate of John
Paul II. (About all of this, I will have much more to say at
Father Neuhaus' Erasmus lecture in New York in
November, so we will leave the rest for then.)

*Fifth:* With John Paul II, the Roman Catholic Church has
entered the ecumenical movement for the long haul, and, in
so doing, has reshaped the quest for Christian unity as a
quest for unity in truth. Similarly, and, in the *sixth* place, the
pope's achievement in the field of interreligious dialogue
and in the Church's dialogue with science, represents an
expression of his conviction that all truth is related to the
One Truth Who is God. Respect for the religious convictions of others without compromising one's own convictions seems, of course, an impossibility to many secular
people – and, indeed, to not a few Christian intellectuals
and religious leaders as well, as the recent controversy over
*Dominus Iesus* has reminded us.

Yet, unless that possibility – unless the possibility of
convictions engaging each other in a common quest for the
truth – can be created, the 21st century will inevitably be
shaped by resurgent religious convictions which are destined for serious conflict. By insisting on religious freedom
as the source and safeguard of all human rights; and by further insisting that the right of religious freedom is tethered
to the obligation to seek and adhere to the truth; and by
teaching as he did in *Redemptoris Missio* that the Church
proposes, rather than imposes – while concurrently teaching that what the Church proposes *is* truth, not a mere

lifestyle choice – by doing all these things, John Paul II has modeled, I believe, an alternative to sectarian violence and state-enforced secularism, and this in a world in which the deepest convictions of human beings are often in conflict, rather than in conversation.

The pope's achievement number *seven* is in Catholic-Jewish relations; in this he has been widely applauded, but not, perhaps, fully understood. John Paul II certainly celebrates, lifts up, and affirms the great progress that has been made in Christian-Jewish relations over the past 35 years. Transformations in our liturgy, in our catechetics, and in our preaching have brought to hundreds of millions of Catholics around the world a new consciousness of their debt to the people of Israel and of their unique relationship to living Judaism. However, at least some of our partners in that dialogue over the past 35 years imagine that we have reached the end of the agenda; that with Catholics and Jews now working together in America, for example, to insure a tolerant society and an open public square, that pretty much completes the agenda.

The Pope has a much, much bolder idea in mind. He believes – so I believe – that the past 35 years have been an occasion to clear out the rubbish, if you will, of some 1900 years of an often-tortured relationship in order to get to the real agenda, which is religious in character. And, I think that, because of his accomplishment here, faithful Catholics and faithful Jews are now on the edge of a new conversation – a new theological conversation of a sort unimaginable since the parting of the ways between the budding Christian movement and what became Rabbinic Judaism more than 1900 years ago. If in the 21st century, or the 22nd century, or the 23rd century, Christians and Jews begin talking together again about election, covenant, and the common moral border we share in the Ten Commandments – and perhaps even about our common Messianic hope – then that re-ignited religious conversation, that theological conversation renewed after a hiatus of almost two millennia, will be in large part because of what this pontificate has accomplished, in response to the teaching of the Second Vatican Council in *Nostra Aetate*.

This is an accomplishment that has tremendous implications for inter-religious dialogue and also, I would suggest, has great public implications as well. If these two peoples have the responsibility to carry those Ten Commandments, that law code, for a people who would not wish to fall back into the habits of slaves, into the public square, then they have the responsibility to be talking to each other about the meaning of the Decalogue as a code for a people wishing to be human in the fullest sense of the term.

*Eighth*, in the long view of cultural history, I think it will prove to be the case that the sexual revolution of the 20th century was yet another expression of a deficient and defective *humanism* tied to another deficient and defective concept of freedom – in this case, freedom understood as the right to pursue the pleasure principle so long as no one or no one in whom the state asserts a compelling public interest gets hurt.

The Christian response to the sexual revolution has not, I think we must admit, been very impressive. Much of liberal Protestantism simply surrendered to it. *Humanae Vitae*, for all of the truth that it carried – and it did carry the truth – was not, we have to admit, a very pastorally successful attempt to address the basic issues. I would suggest, though, that John Paul II's theology of the body, contained in those 130 remarkable Wednesday audience addresses given between 1979 and 1984, is both the *eighth* great achievement of this pontificate and, quite arguably, the most creative Christian response to the sexual revolution ever articulated. Its insistence on the sacramentality of the human body, and the sacramentality of sexual love, is a profoundly Catholic and necessary challenge to the new gnosticism that undergirds the sexual revolution.

John Paul II's teaching that our embodiedness, and the mutuality built into it, express deep truths about the world, and teach us important things about the world's Creator, and, indeed, about the interior life of God himself, gives us, I believe, compellingly powerful grounds on which to say to *Playboy* and *Cosmopolitan* and all the rest: human sexuality is far, far greater than you imagine! We are the ones who take seriously our embodiedness, our sexual embodiedness. You are the ones who are reducing this to another contact sport. There is a tremendous challenge for people like us, Catholic intellectuals, Catholic scholars, Catholic teachers: we need to translate the theology of the body into catechetical materials, homiletic materials, seminary materials, college and university materials, for the next century. This is the issue on which the cultural war is being fought most passionately, but with the theology of the body, I believe, the pope has given us the weapons – the intellectual weapons and, indeed, the pastoral weapons – to engage this cultural war on much firmer ground than many Catholics have seemed to be able to engage it in the past.

I am quite struck when I go around to campuses these days, including, for example, the campus of Smith College, where I was last April, not expecting to have this idea well received. Yet the degree of interest in this remarkable set of teachings of the pope, particularly from young women who are, after all, the primary victims of the craziness of the past 35 years, was itself remarkable. So I would like to lay that challenge on you, perhaps for you to raise with your students in the years ahead. We have here a body of material of tremendous power waiting to be unleashed; and we need to translate it into a reader-friendly, user-friendly, catechetical, homiletic, and teaching forms.

Finally, I would like to say that the achievements of this pontificate, the enduring achievements, can only be measured one by one and from the inside out. Tens of millions of people around the world in a bewildering variety of cultural contexts have been inspired to live out, in their own lives, the consequences of the challenge that John Paul II posed to the Church and to the world on October 22, 1978. The challenge was: "Be Not Afraid!" When the new pope said that, when he said that in that great inaugural homily of his, surely some were tempted to think of this as the most fragile kind of romanticism.

Yet for nearly 22 years, we have been watching this remarkable human being – whom we believe to be the successor of St. Peter, the Vicar of Christ – living out the meaning of all this in his own life, constantly emptying himself of himself in order to give courage to others. All this has had, I believe, a stunning impact on the world, the implications of which we cannot really measure, because we're talking about the interior lives – the souls – of tens of millions of people around the world. The summons to live without fear, to live beyond fear – because all of our fear was nailed to the cross with Christ and transformed in the Resurrection – has not only changed innumerable lives, it has changed the course of history. This is the *ninth* and greatest enduring achievement of John Paul II.

Who knows what others may do? Who knows what *we* may do if we have the wit, the will, and the nerve to carry on the message of Christ-centered fearlessness in the Church that has emerged from the pontificate of John Paul the Great? Who knows? Thank You.

George Weigel, a Senior Fellow of the Ethics and Public Policy Center, is a Catholic theologian and one of America's leading commentators on issues of religion and public life. A native of Baltimore, he was educated at St. Mary's Seminary College in his native city, and at the University of St. Michael' s College in Toronto.

He is the author or editor of some fifteen books, including *Catholicism and the Renewal of American Democracy* (Paulist, 1989), *The Final Revolution: The Resistance Church and the Collapse of Communism* (Oxford, 1992), and *Soul of the World: Notes on the Future of Public Catholicism* (Eerdmans, 1994). He has also contributed essays, op-ed columns, and reviews to major opinion journals and newspapers in the United States, and has also appeared on numerous radio and television programs.

In his role as a Senior Fellow of the Ethics and Public Policy Center, he prepared a major study of the life, thought, and action of Pope John Paul II, entitled *Witness to Hope: The Biography of Pope John Paul II*, which was published to international acclaim in the fall of 1999 and has been translated into numerous foreign languages.

# JOHN PAUL II ON THE FAMILY

## Elizabeth Fox-Genovese

Not long since, most people took the concept of family for granted even when they did not necessarily take it to signify the same set of human relations. Today, however, the family ranks as one of the most hotly contested of concepts, and debates about its nature and function evoke heated passions in all quarters. The very existence of the debates points to far-reaching and portentous changes in the most fundamental understandings of the human condition, notably, the relations between the individual and the community; the claims of sexuality and desire; the proper understanding of woman's nature and vocation; the relations between women and men; and the mutual relations and responsibilities of parents and children. And the changes I have evoked here represent but a few of the visible manifestations of a deep sea change in the character and organization of human societies.

None has been more conscious of and attentive to the possible implications of these changes than Pope John Paul II. Memorably in *Crossing the Threshold of Hope*, but throughout his writings, he has depicted our times as a struggle between the Culture of Life and the Culture of Death. In this spirit, he has unremittingly insisted upon the centrality of the family in the waging of the struggle and its outcome. From the early days of his pastorate in Poland until his most recent reflections upon the challenge of the new millennium, he has urged Catholics to understand the family as the necessary grounding and context for the human person. Thus, in 1965, *Gaudium et Spes*, of which he was a primary author, proclaimed: "The well-being of the individual person and of human and Christian society is intimately linked with the healthy condition of that community produced by marriage and family."[1]

Here and elsewhere, John Paul II has underscored a central aspect of all of his teaching, namely, that the personhood of each of us depends upon the recognition of the other – depends, that is, upon the gift of self to the other. The capacity for that self-gift, quintessentially embodied in the relations of God the Father and God the Son, can only be developed in the intimacy of the binding commitment of husband and wife and of parents and children. Thus, should the binding commitments erode the intimacy and trust they alone can cultivate, the fullness of personhood will erode as well, and we will confront a world of self-seeking antagonists.

This concern for the family as the fundamental custodian of life amidst an encroaching Culture of Death has always figured at the center of Pope John Paul II's theology, philosophy, psychology, anthropology, and social teaching. Commitment to the strengthening of families in a world that tends to tear them apart has always ranked high among his sense of pastoral responsibilities. In 1967, as archbishop of Kraków, he organized an intensive course on marriage preparation and family issues for thirty priests and sixty lay people. The course, which met at his residence and lasted for a year, explored a range of intellectual, pastoral, and practical issues. In 1968, he built upon this initiative, creating the Division of Family Pastoral Care within the Metropolitan Curia, and in 1969, he established an archdiocesan Institute for Family Studies, which became the intellectual training ground for the Division of Family

---

1. Pastoral Constitution on the Church in the Modern World: Gaudium et Spes, promulgated by His Holiness, Pope Paul VI on December 7, 1965 (Boston, MA: St. Paul Books & Media, 1965), 48.

Pastoral Care, and which sponsored conferences on issues such as the theology of marriage, child care, and the healing of post-abortion grief.

By the 1970s, the Institute had established an affiliation with the Pontifical Faculty of Theology, and had evolved into a two-year program to train seminarians, priests, and lay men and women to serve as instructors and facilitators in the programs to prepare couples for marriage. Archbishop Wojtyla urged all pastors in the diocese to establish such a program.[2] It would be seriously misleading to attempt to minimize the significance of these endeavors in the vision of the man who would become John Paul II – to attempt to marginalize or compartmentalize them as somehow peripheral to his central theological, philosophical, anthropological, and social interests. As George Weigel demonstrates in his masterful biography of John Paul II, the conditions in the Poland of Wojtyla's youth, young manhood, and early clerical career continuously reminded him of the importance of family both as protection against the worst onslaughts of Nazism and Communism, and as the core building block of any decent and humane – any truly Christian – society. In this respect, Wojtyla's dedication to the ideal and the practical reality of family constitutes a foundational element of his understanding of the meaning and mission of Catholicism during the closing decades of the second millennium and the beginning of the third.

Wojtyla's preoccupation with the family derived directly from his theological, philosophical, and psychological understanding of the human person, which he articulated – albeit in somewhat different fashion – in his two doctoral dissertations. The first, completed in 1948 at the end of his two years at the Angelicum in Rome, *Doctrina de fide apud S.*

<hr/>

2.  George Weigel, *Witness to Hope: The Biography of John Paul II* (New York: HarperCollins, 1999), 196.

*Ioannem a Cruce* (The Doctrine of Faith According to Saint John of the Cross), explores the mystical dimension of each person's encounter with God and emphasizes that the very substance of personhood derives from the communion between the person and God: "We cannot know others unless we know them as persons called to communion with God" – which means that "whoever takes God away from human beings is taking what is deepest and most truly human in us."[3]

Wojtyla wrote his second thesis for the doctorate he completed after his return to Poland. Entitled *An Evaluation of the Possibility of Constructing a Christian Ethics on the Basis of the System of Max Scheler*, the thesis assessed the value of Scheler's phenomenology for Catholic thought. Wojtyla appreciated the potential contribution of phenomenology to an understanding of the human experience, but he insisted that it would end in solipsism if not grounded in "a general theory of things-as-they-are."[4] The study marked his attempt to link the objectivity of philosophy with the subjectivity of individual experience, and it manifested his characteristic tendency to reconcile or connect apparently opposing aspects of thought and experience, as in his book, *Love and Responsibility*, which appeared in 1960.[5] *Love and Responsibility* moves into the realm of specific relations among human beings, notably between women and men, and argues forcefully against "situationism" and existentialism, both of which promote the tendency to use other

---

3.   This theology, Weigel insists, contains the essential elements of Wojtyla's subsequent writings and "defined the line of battle on which, for forty years, he would contest with communism for the soul of Poland." Weigel, *Witness to Hope*, 69.

4.   Weigel, *Witness to Hope*, 111.

5.   Karol Wojtyla, *Love and Responsibility*, (rev. ed. New York: Farrar, Strauss & Giroux, 1981; orig. ed., 1960).

human beings as objects. In discussions of sexuality, chasti-
ty, and vocation, Wojtyla insists upon the imperative of
mutual recognition and respect between a woman and a
man as the foundation of marriage and, by extension, of the
family.

As an active participant in the Second Vatican Council,
Wojtyla played a major role in the drafting of *Gaudium et
Spes* (Pastoral Constitution of the Church in the Modern
World). *Gaudium et Spes* emphasizes the ways in which the
modern world offers man unprecedented opportunities
and unprecedented dangers – new forms of freedom and
new forms of slavery. With the dramatic triumph of indus-
trial life over rural life, "the human race has passed from a
rather static concept of reality to a more dynamic evolu-
tionary one," and this transition has confronted us with a
daunting array of new problems – problems that must ultimately be understood as a crisis of humanism.[6]

Emphasizing the importance of marriage and family as
the bedrock for people who attempt to respond to this crisis, Wojtyla also acknowledges that the "excellence" of
marriage as an institution "is not everywhere reflected with
equal brilliance, since polygamy, the plague of divorce, so-
called free love, and other disfigurements all have an
obscuring effect."[7] Marriage and the family have suffered
innumerable pressures and have often – some would claim
more often than not – failed to realize their highest mission.
Nothing in Pope John Paul II's writings, before or after his
ascension to the papacy, suggests that he is naïve about the
multiple variations in marriage and family throughout the
history of the world. He nonetheless insists that the "inti-
mate partnership of married life and love has been established by the Creator and qualified by His laws and is root-
ed in the conjugal covenant of irrevocable personal con-

6.    *Gaudium et Spes*, 7.
7.    *Gaudium et Spes*, 48.

sent." Thus, he continues to leave no excuse for misunder-standing: "God Himself is the author of matrimony, endowed as it is with various benefits and purposes."[8]

From Wojtyla's early years as a priest, he had an imme-diate grasp of the social and political forces that threatened the solidity of marriages and family life. Initially, he recog-nized the threat in the Communist intervention into family life and, especially, the Communists' hostility to the sacra-mental character of marriage. Subsequently, however, he has become increasingly sensitive to the ways in which the wealth of the developed world and the globalization of the economy are threatening the integrity of marriage and fam-ily life.

In the most highly developed nations, secularism has besieged traditional belief in any form of divine or natural authority, thereby undermining the very notion that any authority – including the authority of parents over children – may legitimately limit the freedom of individuals. At the same time, and arguably in response, within the developed nations and, more intensely, beyond their borders, religious fundamentalism has been strengthening its hold upon peo-ples who vehemently reject what they view as the social and cultural corruption of modernity.[9] In different ways and at different rates, both secularism and fundamentalism have contributed to what Pope John Paul II has designated the Culture of Death – a culture that holds human life cheaper and cheaper until it drains it of all intrinsic value, a culture that transforms people into objects or even obsta-

---

8.   *Gaudium et Spes*, 49. For an extensive discussion of John Paul II's views on marriage, see Mary Shivanandan, *Crossing the Threshold of Love: A New Vision of Marriage* (Washington, D.C.: Catholic Univ. of America Press, 1999).

9.   See, for example, Samuel P. Huntington, *The Clash of Civilization and the Remaking of World Order* (New York: Simon & Schuster, 1996) and Bernard Lewis, *Islam and the West* (New York: Oxford Univ. Press, 1993).

cles. This is not a self-portrait that appeals to the affluent denizens of the developed world, who reject the very notion of the Culture of Death, and even more the view of themselves as its purveyors. Caught up in a world overflowing with commodities and armed with a science that promises to extend and even create human life, they find it easy to take their unprecedented material prosperity as the standard for human fulfillment. Nor do the prophets of traditional religion countenance a view of themselves as reactionary and ignorant.

Throughout the globe, multinational corporations are drawing people out of traditional families and communities, binding some individuals to the prospects of new possibilities, while condemning their kin to the dustbins of the cities or the dust bowls of the villages. The greatest – and most awesome – power of the global economy lies in its ability to transform everything it touches and its ability to touch everything. In this respect, it acts as the ultimate solvent of the bonds that shape and guarantee our humanity – our intrinsic worth and dignity as persons. The formidable challenge of our times, as John Paul II demonstrably understands, lies in the defense, reconstitution, and adaptation of those bonds to conform to the valuable aspects of globalization, without succumbing to its destructive tendencies to atomization and commodification.[10]

Amidst the kaleidoscope of changes that have overwhelmed the world during the twentieth century, one may overshadow all of the others, at least with respect to the persistence of families and the quality of our culture, which depends upon their vitality. In contrast to every other society known to human history (with the possible exception of Soviet Russia in the early 1920s), contemporary American society, seconded in varying degrees by other parts of the

10. For an interesting secular appraisal, see Thomas L. Friedman, *The Lexus and the Olive Tree* (New York: Farrar, Strauss, Giroux, 1999).

world, has declared the sexuality of nubile women a matter of indifference. Primary responsibility for this unprecedented development belongs to the sexual revolution of the 1960s and 1970s, although feminists and gay and lesbian activists have enthusiastically promoted it. The advocates of this revolution may not have foreseen that its primary beneficiaries would be men, but their campaign to secure the sexual freedom of women has inescapably liberated men from responsibility to the women whom they impregnate – thereby, with a snap of the fingers, undoing the work of millennia. From the days of the Old Testament until our own, societies had waged a continuing struggle to hold men accountable for the women whom they impregnated and the children they fathered. The sexual freedom of women has made a mockery of those efforts and is effectively abandoning men to their own (frequently destructive and self-destructive) devices.[11]

In this climate, sexual relations have shed even the pretense of communion or covenant, becoming nothing more than the gratification of individual desire, and sexual identities have become nothing more than the temporary prod-

---

11. For a fuller discussion of the sexual revolution and its implications, see Elizabeth Fox-Genovese, *Feminism Is Not the Story of My Life: How the Feminist Elite Has Lost Touch with the Real Concerns of Women* (New York: Doubleday/Nan Talese, 1996); and my *Women and the Future of the Family*, with responses by Stanley J. Grenz, Mardi Keyes, Mary Stewart Van Leeuwen, Eds. James W. Skillen & Michelle N. Voll (Grand Rapids, MI: Baker Books, 2000). For the specific effect of the pill and abortion on men's propensity to marry the women they impregnate, see George A. Akerlof, Janet L. Yellen, and Michael L. Katz, "An Analysis of Out-of-Wedlock Childbearing in the United States," *Quarterly Journal of Economics* CXI (1996): 277–317. It should be noted that Akerlof, Yellen, and Katz write from the liberal rather than the conservative end of the political spectrum. Indeed, President Clinton has recently appointed Janet L. Yellen to the Council of Economic Advisors.

ucts of choice or construction. Many, perhaps most, of those who embrace the tenets of radical sexual liberation find any notion of a sexual nature – a sexuality grounded in nature – offensive, or at least unacceptably constraining. To be endowed from birth with a sexually specific nature, they insist, is the equivalent of imprisonment, especially if that nature includes the ability to bear children and the predisposition to form binding attachments to them. It seems more than likely that the determination to free sexual pleasure from the possibility of reproduction, whether by artificial birth control or abortion, has had an effect exactly opposite to the one intended. The intention had been to protect and extend the pursuit of sexual pleasure, frequently with the professed intent of fostering intimacy between spouses. The result, however, seems to have been a growing tendency to objectify sexual partners, viewed as temporary sources of gratification. When the possibility that the woman might become pregnant – the sign of her unique nature as a woman – is excluded from consideration, an essential aspect of the intimacy between the sexes is lost.

Cultures of all times and places abound with local versions of "the war between the sexes," and the unreflective might be tempted to take them as evidence that the differences that arise from the specific physical embodiments of women and men necessarily lead to antagonism between them. In fact, as often as not, evocations of the antagonism between the sexes are humorous, and they focus upon the ways in which sexual difference may foil understanding of the other: "It's a guy thing" or "It's a girl thing." But beneath the sense of playful jockeying for position lies the deeper recognition that the difference that divides is also the difference that cements women and men into the covenant of marital love and the shared commitment to the children that results from it.

The rebellion against the idea that women are, in an essential aspect of their natures, women, and not men, strikes at the very foundation of civilized society and portends tragic consequences. We all know that the cost to children is high, sometimes disastrously so. We may, however, be slower to recognize that the recognition and union of sexual difference in marriage constitutes the cornerstone of freedom. In this regard, the words of Pope John Paul II in *On the Dignity and Vocation of Women*, merit attention: "*Both man and woman are human beings to an equal degree*, both are created in *God's image*" (#22). Neither, however, can exist alone, but only "as a 'unity of the two,' and therefore *in relation to another human person.*" For both women and men, "being a person in the image and likeness of God also involves existing in a relationship, in relation to the other 'I'" (#25).

Our century has included significant changes in the status and opportunities of women, and most of them have been long overdue. Nowhere is it written that men and women's specific natures entitle men to beat, enslave, exploit, or otherwise abuse women. Our understanding of women's talents and capabilities has changed radically during the past century, as has our understanding of the employments for which women are suited. Today, however, we confront a dangerous polarization that pits traditionalists, who condemn all change in women's situation, against radicals, who insist that the very notion of a distinct female nature is a repressive fiction. The worst consequence of this confrontation is that it has drowned out the voices of those who regard most of the changes in women's situation as beneficial, while continuing to accept the significance of women's embodied being with the unique capacity to bear and nurture new life.

Feminists rage at the pope's claims that "woman's singular relationship with human life derives from her vocation to motherhood"; that "the maternal mission is also the basis of a particular responsibility"; or that "the woman is called to offer the best of herself to the baby growing within her," since "it is precisely by making herself 'gift' that she comes to know herself better and is fulfilled in her femininity" (#26). Many deplore his insistence that women's employment must always respect the "fundamental duty" of the "most delicate tasks of motherhood" (#27). Most do not like the notion that women's rights include any binding duties at all. Rejecting the pope's vision of the responsibilities that accompany women's rights, feminists promote an unrestricted freedom that disconcertingly resembles equal membership in what he has called "the Culture of Death."

The crux of the difference between the feminists and the pope lies in their respective and antagonistic understandings of women's nature and mission. Feminists dismiss injunctions to service, binding obligations, and loving self-sacrifice as so many hypocritical pieties designed to perpetuate women's subordination to men. The pope, in contrast, views them as fundamental Christian precepts that require the compliance of men as well as women. Complication arises primarily because he believes that those precepts apply differently to women and men: no less compellingly to one sex than the other, but differently. Feminists see that acknowledgment of difference as a capitulation to received prejudice. And only the complacent or the unreflective can deny that throughout the centuries the evocation of difference has frequently served to justify women's subordination and to restrict their freedom. Some might find a trace of support for this view in the pope's appeal to Catholic universities and centers of higher education "to ensure that in the preparation of the future leaders of society they acquire a special sensitivity to the concerns of young women" (#61). And, occasionally, words like these do suggest that he may not view women as fit for full participation in the corridors of power and influence – that he expects few, if any, women to figure among society's future leaders.

The experience of recent years has blindingly exposed the agonizing difficulty of attempts to combine responsibility to a family, especially children, with a professional fast track, or even with full-time employment. The pope is effectively arguing that wives and mothers have a moral obligation to put their families first. Feminists argue that women have no greater obligation to do so than men. Unfortunately, when parents struggle over who should be freer to do less, the children get less and less – with ominous consequences for the human and moral fabric of society as a whole. Normally, few would fault his quiet insistence that the abundance of love and peace in the world ultimately depends upon the personal education each child receives in the family. Such education, however, depends upon service – the service of parents, frequently mothers, to children – and upon willingness to forgo or postpone acquisition of the signs of status most valued by the world.

Feminists are not alone in protesting the assumption that women are naturally called to sacrifice ambitions that men are free to fulfill. Many women wonder why they should be called to a service that men and many other women disdain. The pope's recurring demand that the world accommodate women's needs as wives, mothers, and workers, like his insistence upon women's right to equal dignity and opportunity, testifies to his understanding of the difficulties and the pain. But he insists that, to surmount these conflicts, women must cultivate the peace of heart that frees them to be teachers of peace: "Inner peace comes from knowing that one is loved by God and from the desire to respond to his love" (#13).

For Christians, this injunction applies as much to men as to women, but Christian teaching has traditionally held that it applies to them differently. In these writings, John Paul II seeks to reaffirm the difference while he combats the oppressive and exploitative uses to which it has been put. In a corrupt world, his admirable vision remains elusive and formidably difficult to realize. Women will understandably continue to wonder how much they can afford to sacrifice without the assurance of support for themselves and their children. These legitimate worries admit of no easy answers, but, in facing the risks, we might profitably reflect upon the pope's essential message: namely, that the rising tide of the culture of death will not be stayed until individuals, one by one, begin to repudiate its claims upon their souls.

Elizabeth Fox-Genovese is the Eleanor Raoul Professor of the Humanities at Emory University in Atlanta, where she has been a member of the history faculty since 1986. A noted historian, she has done significant research and writing in the area of women's studies. She is the recipient of numerous grants and fellowships, including a fellowship from the Rockefeller Foundation, and grants from the American Bar Association and the National Endowment for the Humanities.

She is the author of six books, including *Black and White Women of the Old South* and *Feminism Is Not the Story of My Life*, which has also been published in German. She previously taught at the University of Rochester and the State University of New York at Binghamton.

# JOHN PAUL II AND THE PUBLIC SQUARE

## Rev. Richard John Neuhaus

The subject is the "liberalism" of John Paul II. It involves an argument that I have been attempting to make for a long period of time, and it has been brought to my attention that, despite the lucidity and convincing evidence marshaled in support of this argument, it has not entirely convinced everybody. So I will try again.

There is a delicious piquancy, you might say, about the joint beatification of Pius IX and John XXIII this fall. Here we have two figures who bring together the configuration of the usual ways in which people think about polarizations in the Church – left, right, liberal, conservative, traditional, progressive, *et cetera:* Pio Nono, as the nemesis or the hero, or John XXIII, as the nemesis or the hero, of your cause, depending upon where you stand!

Pius IX, as is well known, issued the Syllabus of Errors. And you will recall that the 80th error that he pinpointed, namely, the proposition that "the Roman Pontiff can and ought to reconcile himself and come to terms with progress, liberalism, and modern civilization," was very emphatically condemned as an error.

I would agree that it continues to be an error, and indeed a grave error, depending upon how one defines progress, liberalism, and modern civilization. This is really what the great argument is all about in terms of the public square – in terms, that is, of the interactions of moral judgments and religiously based moral judgments, and, more specifically, of Christian moral judgments, and, more specifically yet, of Catholic moral judgments, in the public square – where we continue to have to pose the question of how we ought to order our life together. The great debate is over how we define progress, liberalism, and modern civilization.

There are endless taxonomies proposed by various people about how to figure out today where people stand along the left-right, progressive-traditionalist spectra, as these are also proposed by various people. In a sense it is almost inevitable that people will discuss this question endlessly; it is an essentially taxonomical question of how ideas line up in the public square, ideologically, morally, religiously, and politically. But I would suggest that the Church today, and I mean the Catholic Church – in all the richness of her long and complex tradition, but as most vigorously and convincingly and compellingly articulated today by John Paul II – the Catholic Church today *is* the champion of progress, liberalism, and modern civilization. And as we move further into the 3rd millennium, we all ought to have the sense – and, indeed, we all ought to brace ourselves for everything that is involved in knowing – that we are in the vanguard of progress, liberalism, and modern civilization.

When we speak about John Paul II and how these questions configure themselves in the American public square, we always, of course, run the danger of forgetting that he is the universal pastor. If we take only the main teaching documents – and this has perhaps been, in many respects, the most aggressive teaching pontificate in the history of the Church, or at least one could make that argument – if we take only the main teaching documents, we have to resist the temptation simply to incorporate them immediately in the most applicable way to the American circumstance. For the pope is the universal pastor, and these documents lay out truths for the right ordering of the Church and of the whole world in a very, very comprehensive way.

Still, it is true that, with this pontificate, the United States of America – actually, North America as a whole, but particularly the United States of America, along with the whole American social, cultural, political experiment – has been given the most attentive kind of respect as far as the development of Catholic social teaching is concerned. It has been accorded a respect that is, I believe, unprecedented in the history of the Church. This is something new: in the honing, refining, and articulating of the great truths of the Catholic faith today, as they apply to the right ordering of society, the American experiment has been taken, not simply as some great success, or as simply representing a social and historical milieu that has created a lively and vibrant Catholic Church which serves as a cash cow for many of the other enterprises of the Church universally. I think it is fair to say that this was often the view from Rome about the Church in the United States in the past.

Now, however, there is a sense that there is something of great importance to be learned from the United States that can inform Catholic social teaching. When one speaks of progress, liberalism, and modern civilization today, it is not 1789 or 1792 that is the primary point of reference, but rather the American experience beginning, not simply with the Constitutional founding, but with the Puritan errand into the wilderness. To take seriously the teaching initiatives of this pontificate, and to try to incorporate them into the on-going discussion about America and America's purpose in the world – this, I think, is a faithful exercise of what is described as "inculturation," of incorporating into the particularity of our cultural and political experiment the universal truths which the Church champions.

Then and now, what was called liberalism in Pio Nono's time, the time of the Syllabus of Errors, and what is called liberalism today, are often posited as being against normative moral truth in the public square – certainly as being against religiously grounded moral truth, and, most emphatically, as being against Catholic moral truth. This was much more – how should we say it? – aggressively and abrasively and overtly the case in the 19th century, which was still in the shadow of the French Revolution of 1789 and all that, than it is today. What is happening now is that we are witnessing the Church being aligned in a battle over the definition of the liberal tradition. The Church is in many ways in a much stronger position to do this today than was the case in the mid-19th century, when the Syllabus of Errors was written. Indeed, there is a little remarked line in the Holy Father's reflections in *Crossing the Threshold of Hope,* in which he suggests that the Church is in a stronger and more united position today than has been the case for 500 years, that is, since the schism of the 16th century. I think this is true. It is certainly true in terms of the Church's ability to shape and inform the public square, where the deliberations about the question of the right ordering of our life together go on.

In the 19th century, there were two providentially guided developments that strengthened the Church in two major ways to be a more credible witness to freedom. The papal infallibility definition of 1870 represented a clear example of the freeing of the Church from the dominance of temporal and national and tribal divisions. It was a clear and liberating effort, guided by the Holy Spirit, in order to provide a center, not necessarily of control, but rather of normative conversation, within the life of the Church. The definition of infallibility must be seen as a signal moment in the long history of the Church's becoming a champion of freedom – of the freedom of the Church (or the liberty of the Church, as it is sometimes described). This will become even more important in the future, I expect, as we move into what is described – with maddening diversity and often conflicting scenarios for the future – as "globalization." The universality of the Church, anchored in the continuing apostolic witness of the successors of the apostles in communion with Peter, will become an even more urgent question, and not a less urgent one, in the century ahead.

The other great signal act that provided the Church with greater credibility as a champion of human freedom was, of course, the loss of the papal states. And here, neither Puis IX nor other churchmen can be blamed for not recognizing at the time what a great and liberating thing this was going to be for the Christian Gospel and for the life of the Church. The Church was free from the responsibilities and the culpabilities that inevitably attend temporal power; she was positioning herself through the anguish of the 20th century – the bloodiest, most dehumanizing of all the centuries in human history – to emerge at the end of that century as what she is today, namely, the most convincing and comprehensive and compelling of witnesses to human freedom – and, if you will, to progress, liberalism, and modern civilization!

As the Holy Father says in his 1990 encyclical, *Redemptoris Missio:* the Church imposes nothing; she only proposes. Again: the Church imposes nothing; she only proposes. It was precisely her ability to put her own house in order through the universal ministry, reinforced by infallibility and the new freedom from temporal ambiguities which came with the loss of the so-called papal states, that made this possible.

And what is it that the church proposes? Clearly, what the Church proposes is the Gospel of Our Lord Jesus Christ – the one plan, the one economy, of salvation, as is so lucidly and convincingly set forth once again by the Congregation for the Doctrine of the Faith in the recent declaration, *Dominus Iesus.* The Church proposes the saving Lordship of Jesus Christ; the coming of the Kingdom of God; the purposefulness of history; vindication of the human struggle; and the anticipation of that Kingdom and that vindication in the life of the Church herself. The Church is the Sacrament to the world, the prolepsis of what is to be when the truth of *Dominus Iesus* becomes evident to all and "every knee shall bow and every tongue confess," as St. Paul says, "that Jesus Christ is Lord." This is what the Church proposes most importantly; this is the heart of the matter.

For the public square, for the right ordering of our common life, the Church today also makes proposals with an intensity, with a vigor, and with a convincing force of argument that is unprecedented, I think, certainly in the modern era. Certainly, there is no other institution, there is no other voice in the world today, that is within any distance of possessing the degree of the persuasive force or the credibility and influence of the Catholic tradition, now most convincingly articulated by John Paul II. Here the Church in the public square proposes human rights, religious freedom, democratic polity, and a political economy, as the Holy Father says in *Centesimus Annus,* that includes all within the circle of productivity and exchange.

In short, as far as the public square is concerned, I think it is true to say that this pontificate has made it clear that John Courtney Murray has been vindicated in his essential thought. There are many, many criticisms that have been made, and can be made, about Father John Courtney Murray. But his basic argument about the compatibility, and, indeed, the mutually reinforcing dynamics of Catholic social teaching, with what he called the American proposition, has been vindicated very dramatically and beyond any reasonable doubt in the further development – the dramatic further development – of Catholic social teaching in the pontificate of John Paul II. This American proposition, of course, has to be understood as one firmly grounded in truth, as in, for example, "We hold these truths. . . ."

Today we look to the great achievements of the liberal tradition, especially the liberal political order. It is very easy to fall in love, as perhaps Father Murray tended at times to do, at least in his early years, with the high promise and, indeed, the great achievements of the American proposition. Today we know that the contestation over liberalism, and how it is to be defined, becomes more intense with every passing week and every passing year.

Back in 1967, I wrote an article in *Commonweal*. This was before the *Roe v. Wade* abortion decision of 1973, but while the so-called liberalized abortion debate was heating up in New York, Hawaii, and California. The article I wrote was called "Abortion: The Dangerous Assumptions." I tried to make the argument that the tragedy that was unfolding before our eyes was that the title of "liberal" was being applied to the pro-abortion side; and that this was fundamentally a skewing of the liberalism with which many of us had identified during the 1950s and 1960s, particularly in the civil rights movement under the great leadership of Dr. Martin Luther King.

But the abortion debate revealed, and subsequently this has become even more evident, that what we have within, what is called "American liberalism," is a divide so deep that it amounts to a kind of schizophrenia. On the one hand, there is the liberalism of ever-expanding the definition of the community for which we accept common responsibility. This was the liberalism of the civil rights movement at its best. But on the other hand, there is the liberalism of narrow self-interest, self-satisfaction, and self-realization – and the devil and whoever else gets in the way take the hindmost! This divide within American liberalism has become most dramatically, most tragically evident in the debate over abortion.

The liberalism with which, 150 years later, responding to Pio Nono, we would want the Church to be identified, is the liberalism of the American founding. It is grounded in truth. It is not the liberalism of John Stuart Mill. It is this other liberalism of his which is at the heart, which is the driving ideological force, also of what the present Holy Father has so aptly described as the conflict between the Culture of Life and the Culture of Death. This other liberalism is essentially the work, more than of any other one person, of John Stuart Mill. I believe Mill's *On Liberty* has become *the* catechism for millions of people who have never read it or never even heard of it. It is in the very air that we breathe, and it has, to a very large extent in the American public square, exercised a kind of hegemony, if not monopoly, over the definition of the liberal experiment.

One simple principle, you will recall John Stuart Mill argued, is sufficient for the ordering of society. And that one simple principle, variously described, is that people should be permitted to do whatever they want, so long as it does not get in the way of others doing what they want. I can do my thing so long as I do not get in the way of you doing your thing. This is what Mill called his one simple principle, and it is, of course, an idea that premises the whole of society upon selfishness and indifference to others. One really doesn't need to care how other people live, what other people do, what they make of their lives, or even how they destroy themselves, so long as they do not get in the way of my living my life, and, if necessary, and if I chose, wrecking my life as I see fit.

Today this doctrine of selfishness and indifference to others, while it is nuanced and qualified in highly sophisticated ways by various scholars, is essentially the doctrine of John Rawls. I believe it is also, essentially and certainly, overtly and clearly, the doctrine of Richard Rorty. It is clearly the doctrine that prevailed in *Roe v. Wade;* and it became even more explicit in the *Casey* decision of 1992. In this decision it became very clear that at least five of the justices were prepared to say that, whether or not *Roe v. Wade* was rightly decided – and only two of them at that point were prepared to say that it was – it had nevertheless so insinuated itself and entrenched itself in the mores of our public behavior that to disrupt it, to challenge the doctrine of selfishness and indifference to others, would have created a social contest and social chaos that would be unacceptable.

The one simple principle of John Stuart Mill is, as I'm sure most of you know, riddled with contradictions and incoherences. One of the more dramatic of these, of course, is that liberals of this variety have never been able to deal with the question of childhood in any way that made sense of it; they have never been able to deal with those who are not only in the minority of years, but who are for whatever other reason of disability not in charge of their lives. We are told that children should be morally educated, and formed, and shaped; but then at some point when they reach adulthood – and, of course, if some of the more progressive elements in international circles today have their way, that point would be pushed farther and farther back until the "rights" of children would finally almost swallow up childhood altogether – but then when they reach adulthood, there is no longer any morality aside from that one simple principle of Mill's. It is a breathtaking proposition: that one should train children for the observance of the norms that demarcate good citizenship, only to discover when they become citizens that those norms no longer pertain!

And, of course, it is also not true, as we know from the current ascendancy of various forms of what is so aptly called political correctness. It is not true that this form of liberalism is tolerant; rather, as we have witnessed on a thousand different fronts, it is very *intolerant* about its one form of tolerance that is based on its one simple principle. The illiberalism of liberalism is not even anything terribly new, in fact. It is right there in *On Liberty* by John Stuart Mill.

The Holy Father, as alluded to earlier, talks in *Centesimus Annus* about how liberal democracy without moral judgment leads to a form of totalitarianism (perhaps of "soft" totalitarianism, but of totalitarianism nonetheless). And that, of course, is there in the beginning of Mill's view of liberalism. He writes in *On Liberty:* "As mankind improves, the number of doctrines which are no longer disputed or doubted will constantly be on the increase. The well-being of mankind may almost be measured," he goes on, "by the number and gravity of the truths which have reached the point of being uncontested and uncontestable. The cessation on one question after another of serious controversy is one of the necessary incidents of a consolidation of opinion – a consolidation as salutary in the case of true opinion as it is dangerous and noxious when the opinions are erroneous."

In short, once John Stuart Mill and those whom he has convinced are in charge, there will be no more questions to be contested, because everybody being as enlightened as they, will agree on all the questions really worth arguing about. This is a form of what the Holy Father means by soft or disguised totalitarianism. We already know the conse-

quences of it; they are all too evident, especially in some of
the most sacred precincts of the American academy and,
certainly, in much of our media. In *Centesimus Annus*, the
Holy Father, you will recall, writes: "Nowadays there is a
tendency to claim that agnosticism and skeptical relativism
are the philosophy and the basic attitude which correspond
to democratic forms of political life. Those who are convinced that they know the truth and firmly adhere to it are
considered unreliable from a democratic point of view,
since they do not accept that the truth is determined by the
majority or that it is subject to variation according to different political trends. It must be observed in this regard,"
John Paul II goes on to say, "that if there is no ultimate truth
to guide and direct political activity, then ideas and convictions can easily be manipulated for reasons of power. As
history demonstrates, a democracy without values easily
turns into open or thinly disguised totalitarianism" (#46).

In other words, it easily turns into the kind of society
described, indeed, praised, by John Stuart Mill in *On
Liberty*. It is a society in which politics has basically ended.
Politics, though, is indispensable. If one looks, I think, for
the best short definition of politics, it's Aristotle's. It consists of free persons deliberating the question, "How ought
we to order our life together?" It assumes, as Christian faith
assumes, that that question will be contested until Our
Lord returns in glory, and "every knee shall bow and every
tongue confess."

Politics is a permanent vocation, though it is not necessarily the most important vocation; but it is a permanent
vocation, one which is necessary to the advancement of the
*humanum*, of the human project itself. When contention
ceases along the lines that John Stuart Mill proposes for his
enlightened society, then politics will have been brought to
an end. The human project itself will then no longer be
capable of enlisting the visions and the convictions and the
hopes of the citizenry, who must always understand that,
just as we are not yet at the Kingdom of God, so we are to
live always in a posture of anticipating new and better

ways – yes, if you will, even more enlightened and more progressive ways – of ordering our life together. The debate over that is an inherent and necessary part of human life.

At the heart of the liberalism that is posited against the liberalism championed by Catholic social doctrine, there is, quite simply, atheism – as the Holy Father again says in *Centesimus Annus* (#13). "It is by responding to the call of God contained in the being of things," he writes, "that man becomes aware of his transcendent dignity. Every individual must give this response, which constitutes the apex of his humanity, and no social mechanism or collective subject" – no matter how enlightened, one might add – "can substitute for it."

The great error of both collectivist determinism and of individualistic license is that their understanding of human freedom is detached from obedience to the truth. "At the heart of every culture," the Holy Father has written, "lies the attitude a person takes to the greatest of mysteries: the mystery of God." In a marvelously lapidary formulation he then writes, "Different cultures are" – What? What are different cultures? "Different cultures are basically different ways of facing the question of the meaning of personal existence, different ways of facing the question of God." And that, of course, is precisely what we are engaged in when we talk about today's culture wars. We are talking here, not simply at a metaphorical level – and God forbid that they should become real wars, armed conflicts – rather, we are speaking about very different, incompatible, and conflicting ways of understanding personal and communal existence in the face of the ultimate realities, and, particularly, in the face of God.

The liberalism that is traced to John Stuart Mill's one simple idea, one simple principle, is, in fact, as relentlessly posited against the moral tradition that we rightly describe as Judeo-Christian, as were the ideas of the Jacobins and of the pseudo-religions proposed by the French Revolution to replace Christianity. John Stuart Mill does not use the rhetoric of a Robespierre or whoever. He is an English gentleman after all. But I think Maurice Cowling's critique of *On Liberty* is quite right when he says: "Mill's book was not so much a plea for individual freedom as a means of ensuring that Christianity would be superseded by that form of liberal, rationalizing utilitarianism which went by the name of the religion of humanity."

Mill's liberalism was a dogmatic and religious liberalism. It was not the soothing night comforter for which it is sometimes taken. Mill's object was not to free men, but to convert them – and to convert them to a peculiarly exclusive, peculiarly insinuating moral doctrine. Mill wished to moralize all social activity. Cowling notes further: "Mill no less than Marx, and no less than Nietzsche, and no less than Compte, did claim to replace Christianity by something better." And in the passage I read earlier, he makes clear that this something better with which Mill would replace Christianity, and all other traditional authorities, could itself never be replaced in turn – because all right-thinking people would agree with the new regime that had been established. This is thinly disguised totalitarianism, as John Paul II remarks – and not necessarily even so thinly disguised!

And yet we know that in making the case today that the most convincing, comprehensive, and compelling arguments for human dignity and human freedom are advanced by the Christian Gospel, and, most specifically, by the Catholic Church, we know that we run up against enormous obstacles in resistance to this. In every text book with which Americans are indoctrinated, from grade school through graduate school, this is considered outrageously counterintuitive. The idea that the Church is the champion of human dignity and of human freedom, and of all that is best in the achievements of the liberal tradition – this idea goes against everything Americans have been taught.

Here we come most strongly to the whole question of tolerance. It is a necessary question. There are a great many conservatives I know who delight in saying that tolerance is not a virtue, and certainly not a Christian virtue. I think that's wrong. It's not a part of the Christian vocabulary; but if it means that we have a deeply and, indeed, ultimately, grounded reason and obligation to engage others with a respect, and indeed, a reverence, based upon our understanding of them as bearers of a life destined from eternity to eternity, if that is what it means – and that *is* what tolerance in its most serious expression means – then, indeed, it is not only a virtue, it is an indispensable virtue for a humane society.

The great issue is posed by Alan Wolfe, who, most improbably, has been appointed the head of the Institute on Religion and Public Life at Boston College, even though he has written endlessly over the years that religion has no place in public life. Be that as it may, I'm sure Boston College knows what it's doing. Alan Wolfe and I have discussed this issue at times, and he puts it very simply. He says: "Richard, for all your talk about human dignity and all that, the fact is that my liberalism" – and his liberalism is emphatically that of John Stewart Mill, the liberalism of the one simple principle – "the fact is," he says, "that my liberalism can provide a secure place for you in society, but your liberalism cannot provide a secure place for me." He means, in his case, as an atheistic Jew. And, of course, that is a very good way of putting the question.

But he is quite wrong. And the future of Catholic activism, of Catholic arguments, and of the Catholic intellectual life, as they impinge upon the public square – the future of all these things is going to turn very, very importantly on whether or not we can make a more convincing case for tolerance rightly understood, for mutual respect, and for providing a secure – a more secure – place for "the other." I remember years and years ago, back in the 1960s in New York City, the Urban League, which then was a major force, had distributed buttons that many of us wore. And the buttons simply said, "Give a damn." Not very clerical, I admit; but anyway, I wore one. The button meant "give a damn" about racial justice, about poverty, about urban housing, *et cetera* . . . Give a damn. And I recall a curmudgeonly old fellow in our neighborhood who looked at it one day, and said, "Why the hell?" He had a very, very good point. It is by no means self-evident why we should care for other people; and, especially, why we should care about other people when they are very inconvenient and a drag on the society; and when, by any rational calculation of benefit and cost, we'd be better off without them.

Or when they are very, very small and do not come along at the right time. Or when they are very, very old and do not go away at the right time. Why do they still have a claim? Why should we not obey John Stuart Mill's one simple principle? Now, of course, he and others would answer: because it is in our self-interest to do so. To assure that there are those rules in place and those laws in place that allow us to do whatever we want to do as long as we don't interfere with other people doing what they want to do.

But is it really in our self-interest when we can get away with it? When we can get away with violating the rights of others, and, indeed, marginalizing others? We don't have to get hypothetical, for historical instances abound of people getting rid of others when they can get away with it, and when they do not see that it is going to cost them anything, in cases, that is, in which there is no reciprocity in the injustice. I do not think that in John Stuart Mill's society of thinly disguised totalitarianism any convincing answer can be given to the question, "why give a damn?"

I believe that – call it natural law, call it general revelation, call it whatever you want – human beings are wired for knowing. There is a kind of web of mutual obligation and accountability, which has developed at the best and strongest and most persuasive level of progress, liberalism, and modern civilization. It has been developed in documents such as Pope John Paul II's *Evangelium Vitae (The Gospel of Life)*.

We can make the argument that not only is there a reason for caring, but that we ourselves, as a community, must become the exemplars of that caring – though not just in a way that can cheaply be dismissed with slogans like "compassionate conservatism." But we should not sneer at such slogans, either. They are trying to get at something. As with the talk about tolerance, they are trying to get at something that will break the hegemony, challenge what sometimes appears to be a liberal monopoly on the language of progress, on the language of compassion, on the language of civilization and human freedom.

We have much the better argument, however. Our task in the public square, and I think this is what the Holy Father has so energetically given himself up to, is to do nothing less than to renew politics. To renew politics. We should have no illusions, in the manner of John Stuart Mill or the Marxists – or of any of the others who are subject to utopian dreams – that there is ever going to arrive a time in which we will not be contending and deliberating over how we ought to order our life together. This kind of contention and deliberation will go on until Our Lord Jesus Christ returns in glory. This is the task, then: nothing less than to renew politics. It is the only conclusion, the only satisfactory conclusion, for the whole argument. We must settle for no proposed solution to all these questions before then.

Meanwhile, the Church – the Catholic Church led by John Paul II these last 22 or going on 23 years now – has both represented and exemplified the genuine renewal of politics, of deliberating about how we ought to order our life together. We do not want, as the proponents of the one simple principle want, to dominate and to control the conversation. We do not want a state that is a confessional state. We want a confessional society. I believe that the dramatic developments in Catholic social teaching in this pontificate have helped us to understand the state as simply one institution among many in the right ordering of society. It is a very important and even indispensable institution, but it is still simply one institution among others, instrumental to helping all of the centers of "acting persons in community," as Karol Wojtyla would say – persons from the various spheres of sovereignty within society: families, voluntary associations, most of all, communities of ultimate allegiance in worship. All of these institutions must also play their part in a right ordering of a society in which the state does not have the last word. Indeed, as *Gaudium et Spes* discusses, the state is not competent to deal with some of the more – some of the most – important questions. Our understanding of religious freedom, and therefore of freedom at its deepest level, and in all of its dimensions, is grounded in a profound awareness of a Sovereignty that transcends the sovereignty of the state, a Sovereignty that is expressed, above all, in the Gospel of Jesus Christ; but it is also one that is also capable of being known and expressed and acted upon in the conscience of every human person, created as an acting agent in the dignity that God has bestowed upon us.

We do not want the state just to grant the Church certain freedoms. The Holy Father told the bishops of Cuba a couple of years ago, during that most remarkable week when he was there: "The Church is not asking for a gift. She does not ask for a privilege or a permission dependent upon contingent situations or political strategies, or on the will of the authorities. Rather, she demands the effective recognition of an inalienable right." He spoke even more strongly against the notion of a confessional state to the Parliament of Europe in 1988: "Our European history," he said, "clearly reveals just how often the boundary between what belongs to Caesar and what belongs to Christ has been overstepped in both directions. Medieval Latin Christianity, to take but one example, and despite the fact that it evolved the natural concept of the state, hearkening back to the great tradition of Aristotle, fell into the intregalist trap of excluding from the temporal community all those who did not profess the true faith. Religious intregalism, which does not distinguish between the spheres of influence of faith and civil life, and which is still practiced today in other parts of the world, is incompatible with the spirit of Europe, as it was forged by the Christian message."

We do not want any privileges; certainly we do not want any kind of coercive control. We do not want a confessional state but a confessional society. And this confessional society depends upon the evangelization and the re-evangelization that the Holy Father has called for so often and so urgently. If this happens, then the arguments will continue, yet we will still agree with Pius IX when he denied that the Roman Pontiff can and ought to reconcile himself and come to terms with progress, liberalism, and modern civilization. We will say: "That's exactly right."

More than a century later, there arose another pope who challenged the way in which those words were defined – progress, liberalism, and modern civilization. Like St. Paul at the end of 1 Corinthians 12, this pope said to the world, "I will show you a still more excellent way." And allied with innumerable people hungry for truth, a truth far transcending that debased and debasing one of Mill's simple principle, the world began to listen.

Maybe, depending in large part upon people like you and me, and on meetings like this – isn't it a most invigorating time to live? – maybe somebody should write a book called *The Catholic Moment*, taking in all of its seriousness what is contained in that proposition found in John Paul II's *Redemptoris Missio (The Mission of the Redeemer, #39)*: "The Church proposes; she imposes nothing." She only proposes, but what a proposal! What a proposal!

Father Richard John Neuhaus is acclaimed as one of the foremost authorities on the role of religion in the contemporary world, and is President of the Institute on Religion and Public Life, a non-partisan, inter-religious research and education institute located in New York City. He is also Editor-in-Chief of the Institute's monthly publication, *First Things: A Monthly Journal of Religion and Public Life*, one of the most influential contemporary journals. Born in

Canada, Father Neuhaus received his formal education in Ontario and in the United States; he is a graduate of Concordia Theological Seminary in St. Louis, Missouri.

Among his better known books are *Freedom for Ministry; The Naked Public Square: Religion and Democracy in America; The Catholic Moment: The Paradox of the Church in the Postmodern World; Doing Well & Doing Good: The Moral Challenge of the Free Economy*; and, with Rabbi Leon Klenicki, *Believing Today: Jew and Christian in Conversation*.

In 1995, Father Neuhaus edited, with Charles Colson, *Evangelicals and Catholics Together: Toward a Common Mission*. His *The End of Democracy* appeared in 1997, and *Appointment in Rome: The Church in America Awakening* in 1998. Early in the year 2000 appeared *The Eternal Pity* and *Death on a Friday Afternoon: Meditations on the Last Words of Jesus from the Cross*.

# FAITH AS A PREAMBLE TO REASON

## Janet E. Smith

Throughout his pontificate Pope John Paul II has been a tireless defender of human life against legalized abortion and euthanasia, an avid promoter of Natural Family Planning (NFP), and, more recently, a determined opponent of capital punishment. The most magisterial document about the life issues is, of course, his 1995 encyclical *Evangelium Vitae* (on the Gospel of Life). A key and striking term of the document, "the Culture of Death," is one that is used with some regularity even by the media; I heard it several times in reports on the massacre at Columbine High School.

In February of this year, the Vatican sponsored a fifth-year celebration of *Evangelium Vitae*. In a very short speech the Holy Father could hardly have done more to stress the importance of the encyclical. He noted that the fifth anniversary was "taking place within the framework of the Jubilee Year celebrations and is meant to be in prayerful harmony with the pilgrimage I will make to the Holy Land next month to venerate the places where 'the Word became flesh'"(Jn 1: 14).[1] Surely not totally coincidentally, on March 25th of this year, John Paul II could be found celebrating the Feast of the Annunciation Mass at the Basilica of the

---

1. February 14, 2000; I found a copy of this address at: *http://www.priestsforlife.org/magisterium/papal/evanniversary00-02-14.htm*

Annunciation in Nazareth, the day on which *Evangelium Vitae* was fittingly promulgated.

Not only did the Holy Father signal the importance of the document by placing it in the context of the Jubilee year and his historic visit to the Holy Land, his greeting to the participants made explicit his own estimation of the importance of *Evangelium Vitae*; he said:

> I greet all of you participating in this reflection on a document that I consider central to the whole of the magisterium of my pontificate and in perfect continuity with the encyclical *Humanae Vitae* of Pope Paul VI of venerable memory.

Yet in spite of the fact that John Paul II has identified *Evangelium Vitae* as central to the whole of the magisterium of his pontificate, I suspect that it has received much less attention from dissenters by comparison with the frenzy of responses given to *Veritatis Splendor*. And I think *Fides et Ratio* was similarly neglected. One wonders if the energies dissenters spent attempting to undermine *Veritatis Splendor* depleted their resources. Certainly, *Evangelium Vitae* requires an enormous amount of energy; it is written with great rhetorical and philosophic passion, and any attempt to reduce the document to a few disputable points does both the document and the reader severe injustice. In fact, I will need to fight constantly the temptation to confine myself to quoting passage after passage since the document is so powerfully reasoned, supported, and written. Perhaps, dissenters believe, and somewhat understandably, that if once they have jumped ship by rejecting *Veritatis Splendor*, there is no point in showing the unseaworthiness of what they see as weak attempts to shore up a sinking ship. The problem, of course, is that the ship, or bark of Peter, just keeps on advancing towards its destiny. The destiny, it seems, of John Paul II's pontificate is to provide us with the fullest possible restatement of the faith in light of Vatican II and in respect to the "signs of the times."

In *Choosing Life: A Dialogue on Evangelium Vitae,*[2] a compilation of papers given at a conference on *Evangelium Vitae* at Georgetown – and one that has a welcome mix of dissenters and loyalists – for lack of better words, the authors seem to be primarily concerned with what are called "methodological analyses," that is, with the questions: 1) whether the encyclical is more reliant upon Scripture and Christological narratives than on natural law; and 2) with the status of the teachings of the document – that is, with how binding the teachings of the encyclical are on believers, and how persuasive the arguments might be to unbelievers. There is also some concern with the teaching of *Evangelium Vitae* on specific issues such as abortion, euthanasia, capital punishment, and experimentation on embryos. There is, not surprisingly, almost no discussion[3] on John Paul II's reference to contraception as part of the Culture of Death, one that he allies with abortion as the "fruit of the same tree"(#13).

Of all the life issues, dissenters are most at odds with the Church's teaching on contraception. Their proportionalism enables them to allow that the Church is largely right about abortion and euthanasia, though wrong not to allow for some necessary exceptions; and that the Church is also properly worried about experimentation on embryos, though a bit heartless in sight of the likely medical benefits. Of course, the fact that they judge these actions on entirely different criteria from the Church is itself no small deviation. Dissenters also find the present Holy Father astonishingly prophetic about capital punishment (though perhaps not prophetic enough for them). But they find him and the tradition of the Church absolutely wrong-headed about contraception.

---

2.   Kevin Wm. Wildes, S.J., and Alan C. Mitchell, Eds., Georgetown University Press, 1997.

3.   For a minimal exception see Leslie Griffin's essay, *Ibid*, p. 164.

Yet, note that, in his greeting to the participants of the
5th anniversary celebration of *Evangelium Vitae*, John Paul II
as well as calling *Evangelium Vitae* a "document central to
the whole of the magisterium of my pontificate," he also
spoke of it as "in perfect continuity with the encyclical
*Humanae Vitae* of Pope Paul VI of venerable memory." He
could have as naturally spoken of its continuity with the
*Declaration on Procured Abortion*, the *Declaration on
Euthanasia*, or *Donum Vitae*,[4] for instance, but he chose
*Humanae Vitae*. Why?

Perhaps because *Humanae Vitae* was a truly prophetic
document in that it warned that the widespread use of contraception would pave the way for many other moral problems of society. Section #17 of *Humanae Vitae* stated that
with the widespread use of contraception would come a
general decline of morality, a greater disrespect by males
for the physical and psychological welfare of women,
oppressive government actions concerning family planning
issues, and a tendency to treat the body like a machine in
respect to reproductive issues.

One fascinating way to discern the linkage of the issues
of contraception, abortion, euthanasia, and the new reproductive technologies is to study the court cases dealing
with these issues over the last several decades. I have no
intention of providing an in-depth study here, but I do
want briefly to point out that the linkage of jurisprudential
reasoning in the various U.S. court cases legalizing the sale
of contraceptives, access to abortion, and euthanasia goes a
long way towards confirming the prophetic status of
*Humanae Vitae*.

---

4.  All mentioned by Cardinal Ratzinger in his speech at the consis-
    tory on life issues, the preparatory session for *Evangelium Vitae*,
    Vatican City, April 4–7, 1991. This document is important back-
    ground reading for *Evangelium Vitae*. I found it on the
    internet:*http://www.priestsforlife.org/magisterium/threatstohumanlife.htm#rat
    zinger*

*Roe vs. Wade* legalized abortion in 1973 on the basis of a right to privacy found in the penumbra of the constitution first discovered in *Griswold vs. Connecticut* that legalized the sale of contraceptives across state lines in 1965. Thus, a court case permitting contraception to become more prevalent paved the way for abortion in the same way that a contraceptive lifestyle leads to abortion.[5] The court cases in the nineties legalizing euthanasia[6] draw heavily upon principles established in various court cases having to do with contraception and abortion in the immediately preceding decades; the right to kill the body within a body logically lead to the right to kill one's own body. We find a linkage of these issues both through the principles established in court cases, and also through the lifestyles of those who demand them and have recourse to them. As some of you know, I am convinced that until we cease being a contraceptive culture, we will not cease being an abortive culture; and we will continue to career towards being a culture where euthanasia is widely practiced and where embryos are produced as a set of spare parts.

John Paul II in *Evangelium Vitae* has not only articulated how these issues are linked; he has also disclosed the basic philosophical differences that pit the Culture of Death against the Culture of Life – that make not only contraception appealing but also make abortion, euthanasia and embryo experimentation acceptable practices.

*Humanae Vitae* certainly had manifest predictive power, but the remarkably broader scope and greater depth of *Evangelium Vitae* perhaps points out a lack, and maybe a largely understandable lack, in its parent encyclical: that is, there is some evidence that Pope Paul VI did not fully real-

---

5. See, my "The Connection between Contraception and Abortion," *Homiletic and Pastoral Review* 93:7 (April 1993) 10–18.

6. See for instance, Compassion in Dying vs. the State of Washington, US Ninth Circuit Court of Appeals, March 9, 1995 No. 94-35534 D.C. No. CV-94-00119 19–BJR.

ize how readily the teaching of *Humanae Vitae* would be
rejected. In Section #17, where *Humanae Vitae* predicts the
disastrous consequences should use of contraception
become widespread, the document states that responsible
human individuals "will quickly realize the truth of the
Church's teaching on contraception once they consider the
consequences of contraception and the reasons why individuals use it." One wonders how much wryness there was
in the statement of the encyclical's Section #18 that: "It is
possible to predict that perhaps not everyone will be able to
accept a teaching of this sort easily." The only reason given
for the failure of a wholesale acceptance of the teaching of
*Humanae Vitae* is that: "After all, there are so many critical
voices – broadcast widely by modern means of communi-
cation – that are contrary to the voice of the Church."

In the early portion of *Humanae Vitae*, various factors
such as increases in population, difficulties in raising children arising from the demands of the workplace and of
housing, the changing role of women, a changing view of
human sexuality, and an increased optimism in science and
technology for solving our problems – all these are mentioned as forces making child-bearing less attractive. This is
an impressive list of conditions that militate against the
acceptance of the Church's teaching on contraception, but it
seems notably incomplete compared to the penetrating
analysis of the philosophical commitments of the Culture
of Death identified in *Evangelium Vitae* as antithetical to
Christianity's promotion of the Culture of Life.

That Pope Paul VI confined his speculations about the
too ready acceptance of contraception to the influence of
social phenomena rather than to the philosophic and
anthropologic trends shaping those influences, perhaps
suggests a somewhat inadequate understanding of the culture into which the encyclical was released. Still, perhaps
the gap between the basic tenets of Christianity and the
beliefs of the time were not yet fully discernible. Possibly

we were so busy fighting the Cold War externally that we did not fully perceive the corruption growing within. We did not realize the insidious philosophical views that were taking over the culture. Or one might conjecture that the difference of length in the documents accounts for the difference in thoroughness of analysis: *Humanae Vitae* contains about 10,000 words, and *Evangelium Vitae*, allegedly the longest encyclical ever written, weighs in at 30,000 words. Whatever the reason, *Evangelium Vitae* is a very different document, as one might expect from a document written after the world has become a thoroughly contraceptive and abortive world.

There is no denying that *Evangelium Vitae* has its eyes wide open – they are eyes that have penetrating microscopic vision for discerning the philosophic roots of the Culture of Death, and eyes that have futuristic telescopic vision as far as seeing where the philosophic currents that have led to the Culture of Death are heading. Again, I find *Evangelium Vitae* to be a remarkably philosophical document. Indeed, there is a way in which *Veritatis Splendor*, *Evangelium Vitae*, and *Fides et Ratio* can be seen as companion documents, for they are documents that make a sustained attempt to get to the very roots of things as much in a philosophical as a theological way: *Veritatis Splendor* to the fundamental principles of moral theology; *Evangelium Vitae* to the fundamental problems of the times in which we live; and *Fides et Ratio*, in counseling the necessity of a realist metaphysics, to the fundamental principles of philosophies that would be compatible with faith. And in spite of being a document focused intensely on what might be called "applied ethics," *Evangelium Vitae* is drenched not only with sweeping sociological claims; it is deeply concerned with identifying the philosophical assumptions that have produced and sustain the "Culture of Death."

In fact, the movement of the first chapter of *Evangelium Vitae* involves the progressive uncovering of the roots of the

Culture of Death. The opening meditation on Cain's killing
of Abel locates a murderous instinct in the human heart
that explains the human propensity for death-dealing acts.
Themes of *Evangelium Vitae* are foreshadowed in the way
that the Cain and Abel story is portrayed and portions of
the Cain and Abel story are repeatedly used throughout the
encyclical to relate claims being made to this initial murder.
This first murder is not at the hands of some hostile
stranger; rather it is performed by Abel's own flesh and
blood who is in the grip of the Evil One. Cain's readiness to
attempt to cover up his crime, his claim that he did not
know what happened, depicts the human tendency to use
"all kinds of ideologies" to "try to justify and disguise the
most atrocious crimes against human beings." His defiant
"Am I my brother's keeper?" is linked to man's "refusal to
accept responsibility for their brothers and sisters" (#8).

*Evangelium Vitae* draws upon other passages from
Scripture that speak of crimes of blood as "cry[ing] to God
for justice" and states "whoever attacks human life, in
some way attacks God himself." Cain is rightly punished
for his act, though God does not deal with him in such a
way that he loses his dignity. He exiled Cain; he did not kill
him. Citing Saint Ambrose, *Evangelium Vitae* asserts: "God,
who preferred the correction rather than the death of a sin-
ner, did not desire that a homicide be punished by the exac-
tion of another homicide." John Paul II uses the Cain and
Abel story not just to introduce the themes of *Evangelium
Vitae*, but he also punctuates the narrative of the encyclical
with constant reference to dynamic moments in the story.

For instance, *Evangelium Vitae* uses God's question to
Cain – "What have you done?" – to launch its philosophical inquiry; it invites the people of today to ponder the
question for three purposes, in order:

> To make them realize the *extent* and *gravity* of the
> attacks against life which continue to mark human
> history;

To make them discover what *causes* these attacks and *feeds* them; and

To make them ponder seriously the *consequences* which derive from these attacks for the existence of individuals and of peoples (#10; my division and my emphasis).

*Evangelium Vitae* rightly notes that threats against life have always marked human existence, and it lists some of the characteristic threats; but then it quickly narrows its focus to a consideration of the distinctive and particularly insidious ways that the murderous instinct in man's heart has taken over modern cultures – to the point that they merit being called a "Culture of Death."

Human beings have always committed murder, they have always had abortions, they have always killed those who are inconvenient; but what is new about this behavior is, as *Evangelium Vitae* states, that "these attacks tend no longer to be considered as *'crimes'*; paradoxically they assume the nature of *'rights,'* to the point that the state is called upon to give them legal recognition and to make them available through the free services of health-care personnel"(#11; my emphasis). Not only have we decriminalized vicious behavior, we have blessed it and called it good. This is a constant theme of *Evangelium Vitae* – the startling recognition that crimes have now become rights. The whole of *Evangelium Vitae* is largely devoted to the question posed at the beginning of the next paragraph: "How did such a situation come about?" (#12).

In answering this question, some attention is paid to various existential and political situations that make recourse to violence against life appealing. Of great importance is the claim that there are now veritable "structures of sin" that have produced a "Culture of Death" that is concerned with efficiency over the needs of humanity. A "conspiracy against life" has been launched – examples given are abortion pills, use of embryos for research, and euthanasia. One is not surprised to find the population-controllers identified as among the chief purveyors of death. The Vatican admirably has not confined itself to just sounding the alarm about population controllers; it has itself been a relentless and effective foe of the "population controllers" at various UN conferences. We should not underestimate the contribution that the population control and environmental movements make in advancing the Culture of Death. It also identifies multinational companies whose policies and "loans" may drive poor countries further into debt and make it harder for them to take care of their own.

Nonetheless, for all its practical realism in identifying some of the current manifestations of and architects of the Culture of Death, it is not the political or social conditions driving the Culture of Death that receive the most attention in *Evangelium Vitae*; rather, the bulk of the diagnosis seeks to discover the underlying philosophical causes and to provide some sketch of how to counter those arguments. *Evangelium Vitae* is a marvelous document for illustrating the adage that "ideas have consequences." *Evangelium Vitae* portrays God's question to Cain – "What have you done?"(#18) – as an "invitation . . . to go beyond the material dimension of his murderous gesture, in order to recognize in it all the gravity of the *motives* which occasioned it and the *consequences* which result from it."

And again, *Evangelium Vitae* puzzles over a "surprising contradiction," a contradiction that is the tragic consequence of a "long historical process that has reached a turning point." The Holy Father speaks very positively about the human rights movement and the progress it has made in recognizing the value and dignity of all human beings but finds a "tragic repudiation of them in practice." *Evangelium Vitae* finds the "roots of this remarkable contradiction" in a "mentality which carries the concept of subjectivity to an extreme and even distorts it"(#19). Here

*Evangelium Vitae* is speaking of a view of the human person as one independent of others, whose dignity resides in his autonomy. As noble as this view seems, it falsifies human nature and devalues those who are dependent upon others and diminished in their abilities (that is, virtually all of us). We are not surprised to hear reiterated here Cain's feeble, swinish whine: "Am I my brother's keeper?" *Evangelium Vitae* speaks of the "inherent relational dimension of man" that makes it wrong for him to exercise his freedom in an individualistic way. An extreme emphasis on subjectivity and freedom finally leads to a rejection of objective truth and brings men to making as their chief point of reference "selfish interest and whim." The consequences of this for society are devastating:

> . . . any reference to common values and to a truth absolutely binding on everyone is lost, and social life ventures on to the shifting sands of complete relativism. At that point, everything is negotiable, everything is open to bargaining: even the first of the fundamental rights, the right to life. This is what is happening also at the level of politics and government: the original and inalienable right to life is questioned or denied on the basis of a parliamentary vote or the will of one part of the people – even if it is the majority. This is the sinister result of a relativism which reigns unopposed: the "right" ceases to be such, because it is no longer firmly founded on the inviolable dignity of the person, but is made subject to the will of the stronger part. In this way democracy, contradicting its own principles, effectively moves towards a form of totalitarianism (#20).

I am sorry if I am quoting too much, but I find that paraphrase cannot improve upon the passion of the original. Here *Evangelium Vitae* continues some of the philosophic themes of *Veritatis Splendor*: a perverse sense of freedom leads to a rejection of objective truth, eventually to relativism, and then to totalitarianism – all in the name of fundamental rights.

Again, consider the linkage I drew before between contraception, abortion, and euthanasia. Other issues, such as pornography, could be added to this list. At one time these were all considered to be crimes, but concerns with individual freedom and a diminishing confidence in the knowability of objective truth, led to the reluctant legalization of these evils. Although we did not like these actions or much approve of them, we thought that individuals should be free to make up their minds about them and live in accord with their own values. Soon we were no longer willing to disapprove of the values; all was relative, all opinions and all values were equal, namely, that we are all "entitled to our own opinions, our own values"; it became a kind of mantra. Thus, since we had come to believe that there is no objective foundation for morality, for the outlawing of contraception, abortion, euthanasia, and pornography – but because there was still some opposition to them – legalization was not sufficient for their avid proponents. What once were crimes now came to be considered "rights," and not just legal rights, but fundamental human rights.

The powerful at the UN for instance, resorted to a kind of extortion from weak countries; they wanted to require that poor countries recognize certain fundamental reproductive rights before they would provide them with any economic and even humanitarian aid. But what becomes a fundamental right eventually becomes an obligation. I remember reading in a report on the Beijing Conference on Women by a feminist who said one had to admire the Chinese for their willingness to use "Draconian measures" to control population – and she was specifically referring to forced abortion. So much for individual freedom and choice. Totalitarianism rather than a shared sense of human dignity dictates how our "freedom" must be exercised. We have seen a rapid rise in the number of countries accused of doing forced sterilizations; forced abortions are not uncommon; even involuntary euthanasia has a foothold in some countries. Thus, what were crimes become reluctantly legalized; what were at first acknowledged to be only legal rights, become fundamental rights; and what were labeled fundamental rights, become obligations to be enforced by the state.

*Evangelium Vitae* does not stop with its analysis of the Culture of Death by identifying the distorted view of freedom as the cause of relativism that eventually leads to totalitarianism. Section #21 begins with the statement:

> In seeking the deepest roots of the struggle between the "Culture of Life" and the "Culture of Death," we cannot restrict ourselves to the perverse idea of freedom mentioned above. We have to go to the heart of the tragedy being experienced by modern man: the eclipse of the sense of God and of man, typical of a social and cultural climate dominated by secularism, which, with its ubiquitous tentacles, succeeds at times in putting Christian communities themselves to the test. Those who allow themselves to be influenced by this climate easily fall into a sad vicious circle: when the sense of God is lost, there is also a tendency to lose the sense of man, of his dignity and his life; in turn, the systematic violation of the moral law, especially in the serious matter of respect for human life and its dignity, produces a kind of progressive darkening of the capacity to discern God's living and saving presence.

*Evangelium Vitae* goes on with these memorable lines (again, my apologies for the lengthy quotations, but I simply cannot improve upon the text):

> Man is no longer able to see himself as "mysteriously different" from other earthly creatures; he regards himself merely as one more living being, as an organism which, at most, has reached a very high stage of

perfection. Enclosed in the narrow horizon of his physical nature, he is somehow reduced to being "a thing," and no longer grasps the "transcendent" character of his "existence as man." He no longer considers life as a splendid gift of God, something "sacred" entrusted to his responsibility, and thus also to his loving care and "veneration." Life itself becomes a mere "thing," which man claims as his exclusive property, completely subject to his control and manipulation.

When man views himself as a thing and has no awareness of his transcendent nature, of his eternal destiny, he becomes focused on making this life as comfortable and pleasant as possible. Nature becomes something to be conquered, not something to be revered as the creation of a loving God. *Evangelium Vitae* has no trouble reciting the litany of "isms" to which modern man is prone: the "isms" of secularism, practical materialism, relativism, individualism, utilitarianism and hedonism (e.g., #23). Man wants only to do and have; he is not satisfied only with being. He has no patience for suffering and considers the body an instrument with replaceable parts. Our understanding of sexuality has become particularly warped; as *Evangelium Vitae* states, "sexuality too is depersonalized and exploited: from being the sign, place, and language of love, that is, of the gift of self and acceptance of another, in all the other's richness as a person, it increasingly becomes the occasion and instrument for self-assertion and the selfish satisfaction of personal desires and instincts"(#23). The encyclical goes on to state that procreation becomes an "enemy" to be avoided, and a child becomes a possession or a right.

*Evangelium Vitae* acknowledges that overturning or fighting these views can be overwhelming; and that one can easily despair. It announces that in these times it has no trouble designating as "tragic" (the words tragic and tragedy are used 13 times in the document) that our real hope can only be in Jesus Christ Himself, who is the Gospel of Life. In every way the Gospel is opposed to the values of the Culture of Death. All human life is to be valued simply because it is; suffering in its multifarious forms has meaning. All is a gift from God.

Section #34 of *Evangelium Vitae* is extraordinary; it begins with the proclamation: "Life is always a good." What is extraordinary is that, while it then immediately asserts that "this is an instinctive perception and a fact of experience," it goes on to argue *why* life is a good. It does not seem to have the confidence that *Humanae Vitae* expressed that reasonable individuals will easily accept the truths that it articulates. Moreover, the defense that it gives for the claim that "life is always a good," that it has just called "an instinctive perception," is based first and foremost on Scripture. The beautiful middle portion of *Evangelium Vitae*, to a very great extent, retells salvation history with an emphasis on life being a great gift from God and a depiction of man as the "glory of God." As Father Richard John Neuhaus has stated: "*Evangelium Vitae* is an urgent, pleading invitation to humanity to walk in *Veritatis Splendor*, the splendor of the truth of the risen Christ. The encyclical is an impassioned love letter, pleading with humanity to rise to its destined greatness."[7] This impassioned Love Letter resonates with admiration for the capabilities of man, man in service of life, man who must live the Gospel of Life.

Here I would like to pause for a moment to note and briefly discuss the various lines of ethical analysis employed by the encyclical. As mentioned earlier, several commentators have maintained that the encyclical largely draws upon theological and scriptural resources for its arguments; others find ample use of natural law. With the

7. "The Prophetic Humanism of *Evangelium Vitae*," *Crisis* Online, March 1996. I found this online at: http://www. catholic.net/rcc/Periodicals/Crisis/May96/neuhaus.html

exception of an excellent article by Catherine Kaveny of the Notre Dame Law School,[8] few comment on *Evangelium Vitae*'s use of "rights language" to advance its claims, and I think that is a serious omission in assessing the encyclical. Nor can I find much acknowledgement of the "personalist" dimensions of the encyclical, which are so vividly and phenomenologically employed in the mediations on Cain and Abel. Let it be said, though, that those who try to identify the single or the prominent approach to ethics characteristic of John Paul II are going to be very frustrated, because he is, to say the least, eclectic. This is not to say that he is whimsical or sloppy; careful scholars or diligent graduate students will have to comb the documents to learn if the many strands he draws upon are ultimately compatible, and I suspect they will.[9] But I think what we find in *Evangelium Vitae* is what we would likely find elsewhere, and what is not surprising: John Paul II employs different modes of ethical analysis not because he is signaling some significant shift in Church teaching, but because the subject treated can better be approached or requires a certain mode of analysis.

I have already mentioned that it initially surprised me that *Evangelium Vitae* relies enormously and even preponderantly on scriptural and theological arguments to defend the goodness of life;[10] to defend what, as I just pointed out,

8. In *Choosing Life, op cit.*

9. I have argued for the compatibility of these various strands as used by John Paul II in "Natural Law and Personalism in *Veritatis Splendor*" Chapter 13 in *Veritatis Splendor: American Responses,* edited by Michael E. Allsopp and John J. O'Keefe (Kansas City, MO.; Sheed and Ward, 1995), pp.194–207.

10. For commentary on this feature of the encyclical, see John S. Grabowski, "*Evangelium Vitae* and *Humanae Vitae*: A Tale of Two Encyclicals," *Homiletic and Pastoral Review,* 11:96; I found this article on the internet at: *http://www.catholic.net/rcc/Periodicals/Homiletic/11-96/1/1.html*; and John J. Conley, S.J., "Narrative, Act,

it says is an instinctive perception, something that is one of the primary precepts of natural law and that should be one of the truths most easily known to man. Certainly the life issues are issues that are very approachable and perhaps best approachable through natural law principles, if only because natural law principles are universal and scripture is not. Indeed, many passages of *Evangelium Vitae* assert just that. At the very beginning of *Evangelium Vitae*, we read:

> The Church knows that this Gospel of life, which she has received from her Lord, has a profound and per-suasive echo in the heart of every person – believer and non-believer alike – because it marvelously fulfils all the heart's expectations while infinitely surpassing them. Even in the midst of difficulties and uncertain-ties, every person sincerely open to truth and good-ness can, by the light of reason and the hidden action of grace, come to recognize in the natural law written on the heart (cf. Rom 2:14–15) the sacred value of human life from its very beginning until its end, and can affirm the right of every human being to have this primary good respected to the highest degree. Upon the recognition of this right, every human community and the political community itself are founded (#3).

This theme is reiterated throughout *Evangelium Vitae*: that natural law teaches that life is sacred from its very beginning to its end, and that every man knows this in his conscience or heart. I could cite passage after passage, but I will confine myself to this opening passage, and a similar passage at the close of *Evangelium Vitae*. In fact, the last sec-tion of *Evangelium Vitae*, before the concluding prayer to Mary, returns powerfully to the claim that natural law is something accessible to all men:

> The Gospel of life is not for believers alone: it is for everyone. The issue of life and its defense and promo-

Structure; John Paul II's Method of Moral Analysis," Chapter 1 in *Choosing Life, op. cit.*

tion is not a concern of Christians alone. Although faith provides special light and strength, this question arises in every human conscience which seeks the truth and which cares about the future of humanity. Life certainly has a sacred and religious value, but in no way is that value a concern only of believers. The value at stake is one which every human being can grasp by the light of reason; thus it necessarily concerns everyone. Consequently, all that we do as the "people of life and for life" should be interpreted correctly and welcomed with favor. When the Church declares that unconditional respect for the right to life of every innocent person – from conception to natural death – is one of the pillars on which every civil society stands, she "wants simply to promote a human State – a State which recognizes the defense of the fundamental rights of the human person, especially of the weakest, as its primary duty"(#101).

Natural law is invoked not only at the very beginning and the very end of *Evangelium Vitae*; it is invoked in the central passages where John Paul II seems determined to declare infallible the Church's moral teachings on abortion, embryo experimentation, and euthanasia; he invokes natural law and the conscience (here called the "human heart"). About abortion, *Evangelium Vitae* states:

> I declare that direct abortion, that is, abortion willed as an end or as a means, always constitutes a grave moral disorder, since it is the deliberate killing of an innocent human being. This doctrine is based upon the natural law and upon the written Word of God, and is transmitted by the Church's Tradition and taught by the ordinary and universal magisterium.

> No circumstance, no purpose, no law whatsoever can ever make licit an act which is intrinsically illicit, since it is contrary to the Law of God which is written in every human heart, knowable by reason itself, and proclaimed by the Church (#62).

The next section, Section #63, begins by stating: "This evaluation of the morality of abortion is to be applied also to the recent forms of intervention on human embryos which, although carried out for purposes legitimate in themselves, inevitably involve the killing of those embryos." And Section #65 says about euthanasia:

> Taking into account these distinctions, in harmony with the magisterium of my predecessors and in communion with the bishops of the Catholic Church, I confirm that euthanasia is a grave violation of the law of God, since it is the deliberate and morally unacceptable killing of a human person. This doctrine is based upon the natural law and upon the written word of God, is transmitted by the Church's Tradition and taught by the ordinary and universal magisterium. Depending on the circumstances, this practice involves the malice proper to suicide or murder.

In each of these passages, John Paul II invokes natural law as a source of knowledge available to man for judging the morality of actions.

When we hear John Paul II invoke the natural law, we should never think that he holds to a version of natural law that holds that the heart of natural law is that "natural processes determine morality" (this I believe to be a caricature of natural law created by its opponents). Rather, the heart of natural law is that the essence of things should be respected and that man through experience and reflection can readily know basic principles governing morality (in Thomistic terms, first principles and primary precepts), that is, man can discern which actions are in accord with human dignity. Nor should we hear John Paul II asserting that the moral law is something that is only exterior to man, something that is imposed upon him from the outside.[11] Indeed, we find John Paul II linking his personal-

11. See Martin Rhonheimer, *Natural Law and Practical Reason: A Thomist View of Moral Autonomy*, New York, 2000.

ism with natural law, precisely through his constant invo-
cation of man's conscience. One of the glories of man is his
ability to share in God's providential reasoning. As *Veritatis
Splendor* states, Christianity is neither a matter of a heteronomous law – of a law imposed from the exterior – nor
of a radical individual autonomy. *Veritatis Splendor* tantaliz-
ingly and correctly speaks of a participated theonomy
(#41). The primary place in which to locate this participated theonomy is in man's conscience. John Paul II's choice to
use a sustained deliberation on Cain's killing of Abel
enables him to make concrete and personalize the role of
the conscience in human life, here, in each person's recognition of the value of human life. Consider this passage:

> The sacredness of life gives rise to its inviolability,
> written from the beginning in man's heart, in his con-
> science. The question: "What have you done?" (Gen
> 4:10), which God addresses to Cain after he has killed
> his brother Abel, interprets the experience of every
> person: in the depths of his conscience, man is always
> reminded of the inviolability of life – his own life and
> that of others – as something which does not belong to
> him, because it is the property and gift of God the
> Creator and Father (#40).

Throughout *Evangelium Vitae*, John Paul II treats the
questions addressed to Cain as questions addressed to the
conscience of every man. The sections of *Evangelium Vitae*
that treat of the natural law make multiple references to the
need of each man to act in accord with his conscience and
repeatedly assert that those who consult their consciences
will find a respect for life implanted there:

> The commandment, "You shall not kill," even in its
> more positive aspects of respecting, loving, and pro-
> moting human life, is binding on every individual
> human being. It resounds in the moral conscience of
> everyone as an irrepressible echo of the original
> covenant of God the Creator with mankind. It can be

recognized by everyone through the light of reason
and it can be observed thanks to the mysterious working of the Spirit who, blowing where he wills (cf. Jn
3:8), comes to and involves every person living in this
world (#77).

As we see, John Paul II is confident that all reasonable
men can recognize the inviolability of human life.

Yet alongside of these proclamations of the ability of
man through his reason to discover the sanctity of life, we
find passages that suggest that the Culture of Death has
obscured the truth written on the heart of man. At the very
beginning *Evangelium Vitae* labels as tragic a most devastating consequences of the Culture of Death: a darkening of
the human conscience. In Section #4 we read:

> not only is the fact of the destruction of so many
> human lives still to be born or in their final stage
> extremely grave and disturbing, but no less grave and
> disturbing is the fact that conscience itself, darkened
> as it were by such *widespread conditioning*, is finding it
> increasingly difficult to distinguish between good and
> evil in what concerns the basic value of human life.
> (#4; my emphasis).

More than one generation has now grown up with contraception being as common as aspirin – has grown up
thinking that only some bizarre right-wing and retrograde
Catholics can have a moral problem with contraception.
More than one generation has grown up with abortion clin-
ics on the corner, and with friends and sisters and mothers
who have had an abortion or multiple abortions. The current generation is being bombarded with propaganda
favoring euthanasia and portraying embryo experimentation as the cure to many of the worst diseases. How can
such individuals get in touch with the instinctual perception or the natural law precept that "life is always a good"?

The destructiveness to man's conscience of the Culture
of Death is a theme repeated throughout *Evangelium Vitae*.

In Section #11, after many of the social conditions that have promoted various manifestations of a Culture of Death have been described, it is stated:

> All this explains, at least in part, how the value of life can today undergo a kind of "eclipse," even though conscience does not cease to point to it as a sacred and inviolable value, as is evident in the tendency to disguise certain crimes against life in its early or final stages by using innocuous medical terms which distract attention from the fact that what is involved is the right to life of an actual human person (#11).

Here we learn that, even in the midst of the Culture of Death, we can see some evidence of the force of conscience in our need to use euphemisms for what we are doing. But I wonder if *Evangelium Vitae* is not already out of date; few people speak of a "termination of a pregnancy" anymore, or "products of conception." They talk freely about abortions and dead fetuses without much of a problem. The Culture of Death is advancing so quickly; it has so much become the norm that we hardly need to disguise what we are doing any longer; it all seems quite perfectly acceptable to us.

At this point I am compelled to cite another lengthy but crucial passage: In Section #24, right after *Evangelium Vitae* has identified the most basic misconception at the root of the Culture of Death – the failure of man to acknowledge his creator, the encyclical states:

> It is at the heart of the moral conscience that the eclipse of the sense of God and of man, with all its various and deadly consequences for life, is taking place. It is a question, above all, of the individual conscience, as it stands before God in its singleness and uniqueness. But it is also a question, in a certain sense, of the "moral conscience" of society: in a way it too is responsible, not only because it tolerates or fosters behavior contrary to life, but also because it encourages the "Culture of Death," creating and consolidat-

ing actual "structures of sin" which go against life. The moral conscience, both individual and social, is today subjected, also as a result of the penetrating influence of the media, to an extremely serious and mortal danger: that of confusion between good and evil, precisely in relation to the fundamental right to life. A large part of contemporary society looks sadly like that humanity which Paul describes in his Letter to the Romans. It is composed "of men who by their wickedness suppress the truth" (1:18): having denied God and believing that they can build the earthly city without him, "they became futile in their thinking" so that "their senseless minds were darkened" (1:21); "claiming to be wise, they became fools" (1:22); carrying out works deserving of death, and "they not only do them but approve those who practice them" (1:32). When conscience, this bright lamp of the soul (cf. Mt 6:22–23), calls "evil good and good evil" (Is 5:20), it is already on the path to the most alarming corruption and the darkest moral blindness (#24).

Because of the centrality of the conscience to the establishment of a Culture of Life, *Evangelium Vitae* tells us further that:

In our present social context, marked by a dramatic struggle between the "Culture of Life" and the "Culture of Death," there is need to develop a deep critical sense, capable of discerning true values and authentic needs. What is urgently called for is a general mobilization of consciences and a united ethical effort to activate a great campaign in support of life. All together, we must build a new Culture of Life: new, because it will be able to confront and solve today's unprecedented problems affecting human life; new, because it will be adopted with deeper and more dynamic conviction by all Christians; new, because it will be capable of bringing about a serious and courageous cultural dialogue among all parties. While the urgent need for such a cultural transformation is linked to the present historical situation, it is also root-

ed in the Church's mission of evangelization. The purpose of the Gospel, in fact, is "to transform humanity
from within and to make it new" (#5).

The encyclical concludes farther on, near its end:

The *first* and *fundamental* step towards this cultural
transformation consists in forming consciences with
regard to the incomparable and inviolable worth of
every human life (#96).

Essential to this process of forming consciences is, as
*Evangelium Vitae* states: "to have the courage to look the
truth in the eye and to call things by their proper name"
(#58). But our consciences are in such pathetic straits that
even straight talk will not be able to penetrate the darkness
of our minds – witness, of course, the Supreme Court's
inability to face up to the horror of partial birth abortions.

Many of you will hear echoes here of Q. 94, art. 6 of the
*Prima Secundae* of the *Summa Theologica*. There Aquinas
responds to the question: "Whether the Law of Nature Can
be Abolished from the Heart of Man?" The answer is that in
respect to secondary precepts, "the natural law can be blotted from the human heart, either by evil persuasions, just as
in speculative matters errors occur in respect of necessary
conclusions; or by vicious customs and corrupt habits. . . ."
We cannot be deceived about the first principle of natural
law that good is to be sought and evil is to be avoided, nor
of a primary precept such as "life is a good"; but we can
become confused about abortion, euthanasia, and reproductive technologies because the precepts against them are
secondary precepts, and they can be "blotted from the
human heart, either by evil persuasions . . . or by vicious
customs and corrupt habits," and we have an abundance of
these in our culture today.

John Paul II offers a strange hope to those of us living
in a time when consciences are darkened and unreliable: he
points out that mankind has been here before:

The history of Israel shows how difficult it is to remain faithful to the Law of life which God has inscribed in human hearts and which he gave on Sinai to the people of the Covenant . . . But while the Prophets condemn offences against life, they are concerned above all to awaken hope for a new principle of life, capable of bringing about a renewed relationship with God and with others, and of opening up new and extraordinary possibilities for understanding and carrying out all the demands inherent in the Gospel of life. This will only be possible thanks to the gift of God who purifies and renews: "I will sprinkle clean water upon you, and you shall be clean from all your uncleannesses, and from all your idols I will cleanse you. A new heart I will give you, and a new spirit I will put within you" (Ezek 36:25–26; cf. Jer 31:34). This "new heart" will make it possible to appreciate and achieve the deepest and most authentic meaning of life: namely, that of being a gift which is fully realized in the giving of self. This is the splendid message about the value of life which comes to us from the figure of the Servant of the Lord: "When he makes himself an offering for sin, he shall see his offspring, he shall prolong his life . . . he shall see the fruit of the travail of his soul and be satisfied" (Is 53:10, 11). It is in the coming of Jesus of Nazareth that the Law is fulfilled and that a new heart is given through his Spirit. Jesus does not deny the Law but brings it to fulfillment (cf. Mt 5:17): the Law and the Prophets are summed up in the golden rule of mutual love (cf. Mt 7:12). In Jesus the Law becomes once and for all the "gospel," the good news of God's lordship over the world, which brings all life back to its roots and its original purpose (#49).

I believe that this passage, with its emphasis on our need for "new hearts," explains why *Evangelium Vitae,* which treats of moral issues quite easily evaluated by natural law, depends so preponderantly on Scripture in its argumentation. My emphasis here on philosophy and natural law should not at all suggest that I believe that *Evangelium*

*Vitae* is primarily a philosophic document that relies primarily on natural law arguments to make its case. Rather, as I stated earlier, I believe the opposite to be true: that it relies primarily on Scripture to make its argument, and that such reliance is curious, given that it would be more natural to rely upon natural law.

The question I have been addressing is why John Paul II draws primarily upon Scripture rather than philosophy to do defend human life. Well, certainly the pope has made it one of his goals, one of the many goals that he has fulfilled so spectacularly, to show the scriptural basis of Church moral teaching. And certainly I think that goal goes a long way towards explaining the abundant use of scripture in *Evangelium Vitae*. But I think a further reason is to be found in the Holy Father's sense that our consciences, both individual and societal, have been "progressively darkened," and that we desperately need "new hearts." And those new hearts will only be given to a prayerful, obedient, sacrament-receiving, and self-giving people. The message of *Evangelium Vitae* seems to be that no natural means will enlighten our darkened consciences; and that unless we become full-fledged Christians and evangelize others, the Culture of Death will continue to triumph over the Culture of Life. It is only the person of Christ and the power of his message that can give us the clear consciences and the new hearts that we need to fight the Culture of Death.

Permit me to use a personal experience to illuminate this point. I have been told by my colleagues in secular institutions that it is very difficult to persuade their students about the pro-life message; they are convinced that freedom of choice is the highest good. At the University of Dallas, however, a larger and larger portion of students comes to us each year (and I am told that this is happening at other campuses as well), filled with a love for Christ and His Church, devoted to regular reception of the sacraments, and well practiced in personal prayer and charitable apostolates. They are already horrified at the crimes against life committed in the world today, and they are delighted to learn that philosophy, that natural law, fortifies what they already hold through faith. They have the "new hearts" that our culture needs. I suspect that it will be their witness more than their arguments that will awaken the consciences of our culture. One also suspects that such an awakening will require an heroic witness, maybe even martyrdom. Their faith and grace will be the primary motivating forces that will enable them to take the courageous stands, and perform the courageous actions, that will bring about the Civilization of Love, the Culture of Life, that John Paul II, a true disciple of Christ, so ardently desires; but it will embolden and assist them to know that they are speaking from an objective standpoint, from a position accessible to all persons reasoning well, and not simply from the basis of faith.

Right after the passage requesting new hearts, right in the middle of *Evangelium Vitae*, John Paul II's meditative style becomes less and less expository until he literally bursts into an explicit prayer. As he concludes his scripturally based instructions on the dignity of sanctity of human life, he pauses to reflect upon the crucifixion of Christ. I would like to cite the whole passage here, but I will confine myself to a few lines. He states:

> Looking at "the spectacle" of the Cross (cf. Lk 23:48), we shall discover in this glorious tree the fulfillment and the complete revelation of the whole Gospel of life. In the early afternoon of Good Friday, "there was darkness over the whole land . . . while the sun's light failed; and the curtain of the temple was torn in two" (Lk 23:44, 45). This is the symbol of a great cosmic disturbance and a massive conflict between the forces of good and the forces of evil, between life and death. Today we too find ourselves in the midst of a dramatic conflict between the "Culture of Death" and the "Culture of Life." But the glory of the Cross is not

overcome by this darkness; rather, it shines forth ever
more radiantly and brightly, and is revealed as the
centre, meaning and goal of all history and of every
human life (#50).

At this moment of great darkness, Christ offers us forgiveness and the hope of eternal life. John Paul II goes on to
say: "But there is yet another particular event which moves
me deeply when I consider it. 'When Jesus had received the
vinegar, he said, "It is finished"; and he bowed his head
and gave up his spirit'"(Jn 19:30). John Paul II's mediation
on this passage emphasizes the need for all to live lives of
total self-giving. After this beautiful meditation, he offers a
prayer, a prayer not of petition, but a prayer of thanksgiv-
ing:

> At this point our meditation becomes praise and
> thanksgiving, and at the same time urges us to imitate
> Christ and follow in his footsteps (cf. 1 Pt 2:21). We too
> are called to give our lives for our brothers and sisters,
> and thus to realize in the fullness of truth the meaning
> and destiny of our existence. We shall be able to do
> this because you, O Lord, have given us the example
> and have bestowed on us the power of your Spirit. We
> shall be able to do this if every day, with you and like
> you, we are obedient to the Father and do his will.
> Grant, therefore, that we may listen with open and
> generous hearts to every word which proceeds from
> the mouth of God. Thus we shall learn not only to
> obey the commandment not to kill human life, but
> also to revere life, to love it and to foster it (#51).

Faith and reason and prayer and action must unite to
restore the love of life to our hearts.

Now I am less romantic, more pedestrian, and possibly
more militant than Father Neuhaus, who as I noted, rightly describes *Evangelium Vitae* as a love letter. My immediate
response upon reading the encyclical was that we have
received our "marching orders" for the next many decades,
perhaps for the next century (one hopes not for the next

millennium). We know where the enemy is located: it is in the philosophy and programs of those who violate the goodness of life; we know what the ammunition is: the grace and love of Christ and the precepts of natural law. And we know what we must do: tell the truth, obey the commandments, receive the sacraments, evangelize, and live lives of total self-giving.

Janet E. Smith is Associate Professor of Philosophy at the University of Dallas. She is the author of *Humanae Vitae: A Generation Later* (Catholic University of America Press, 1991); and the editor of *Why Humanae Vitae Was Right* (Ignatius Press, 1993). She has published widely in the areas of virtue ethics and bioethics. She is a regular columnist for *Catholic Dossier*, and has published in a number of other Catholic journals.

She serves on a number of boards, including the *Our Sunday Visitor* Advisory Board and the Baylor University Medical Center Ethics Board. She has received the Haggar Teaching Award from the University of Dallas, the Prolife Person of the Year Award from the Diocese of Dallas, and the Cardinal Wright Award from the Fellowship of Catholic Scholars. Over 200,000 copies have been distributed of her tape, *Contraception: Why Not?*

# JOHN PAUL II AND ECUMENISM

## Most Rev. J. Basil Meeking, D.D.

Back at the beginning of 1979, when Pope John Paul II had been pope for only a few months, I was working in Rome at the Secretariat for Promoting Christian Unity. One morning as I was walking across St. Peter's Square to work, I met another priest I knew slightly. He worked in the Secretariat of State. On this particular morning he stopped, and, not looking altogether pleased, he said to me: "Doesn't this new pope know there are other offices in the Roman Curia besides the Secretariat for Promoting Christian Unity?"

Then he marched on, leaving me feeling rather pleased. Of course the pope has marched on too, leading the Church and the whole Christian world forward on the ecumenical journey.

With the election of Karol Wojtyla to the papacy in October, 1978, a new era began for the ecumenical commitment of the Catholic Church. You have only to read the Holy Father's remarkable 1995 encyclical, *Ut Unum Sint*, in order to see that. No statement comparable in completeness and conviction has come from any other Christian community. I shall refer to it throughout these remarks.

Everywhere today there are strikingly evident, if still incomplete, ecumenical results which bear the marks of the pope's style and personality. There is, first of all, the relationship with the Orthodox Churches, which has taken on worldwide significance. From one point of view, this relationship is tortuous and fraught with difficulties; yet, at the same time, it is intense and unremitting and marked with the kind of love-hatred quality that family relationships can have.

Over the centuries of the second millennium, the basis for this relationship was always there, and, though it wilted from neglect and the distractions of history, the Catholic Church always continued to speak of "the Churches of the East." Vatican Council II and the present Holy Father have enabled us again to grasp the implications of this and begin to act upon them.

Another example of a striking result is the Joint Declaration and Common Statement signed one year ago between the Lutheran World Federation and the Pontifical Council (formerly Secretariat) for promoting Christian Unity. It is an achievement that pushes back the whole weight of history, a symbolic step for all of the ecumenical movement, even if it is true that the Declaration is marked by some ambiguity and surrounded by unresolved issues.

Mention must also be made of the recent report between the Catholic Church and the Anglican Communion, "The Gift of Authority," put out by the International Commission. It is a remarkable statement with real potential. To say, as some authoritative commentators have said, that it tends to veil some differences that still exist, does not diminish its significance, especially as an unexpected sign of hope in the face of the present divisions and theological disarray within parts of the Anglican Communion.

All of these things have deservedly captured the attention of the world press. Equally stirring but less publicized have been the growing closeness and mutual acceptance between Catholics and other Christians locally, where innumerable practical forms of cooperation have become normal. This equally has meant a transformation of relations among Christians, one that has taken place under the active leadership of Pope John Paul II over the last twenty years.

What has the pope done to bring all this about? To begin with, there has been his regular public assurances that the commitment of the Catholic Church to ecumenism is irrevocable. Why should this be necessary? Was not the Vatican II Decree on Ecumenism clear enough? In the abstract, yes. In fact, the enormous euphoria and unreal expectations aroused by the event of the Council, as well as the media hype surrounding it, led many people to think the unity of Christians would come about overnight and without much effort. Too many people, including both Catholics and other Christians, had not really understood the Decree on Ecumenism and its necessary context – which is the Council's Constitution on the Church, *Lumen Gentium*. These people failed to appreciate that the Catholic Church necessarily brings to the ecumenical movement a Catholic understanding which makes demands both on Catholic ecumenists and their dialogue partners.

There could be no shortcuts. Nevertheless many cried, "Shame!" – and accused the Catholic Church of going back on her ecumenical promises. Pope John Paul II decided it was necessary to respond to this attitude, and he did so in a major statement in 1985. He did so again in 1995 in *Ut Unum Sint*. At that time he solemnly assured the world: "The Catholic Church has committed herself irrevocably to following the path of the ecumenical Venture."

John Paul II has backed that up with actions which engage the Church. One was the publication of the *Directory on Ecumenism* in 1993. This is an official document of the Church that states its ecumenical commitment as well as articulating the Catholic principles on ecumenism; and then it sets out directives for putting these into practice, along with many examples of the kinds of things that need to be done. The *Directory* is the indispensable guideline for faithful Catholic ecumenical action; and because of its magisterial status, it also expresses the irrevocability of the Church's ecumenical engagement.

On an immediately practical level, Pope John Paul II has committed major resources of personnel and money to the ecumenical work of the Church. A large amount of this has gone to launch and sustain the international theological dialogues – both the Catholic participation in the multilateral dialogue of the World Council of Churches' Faith and Order Commission, and the bilateral dialogues which the Catholic Church is carrying on today with nine world Christian communities such as the Orthodox Churches, the Anglican Communion, the Lutheran World Federation, the World Alliance of Reformed Churches, and so on.

Because of the ecclesial self-understanding expressed in the Catholic principles on ecumenism, theological dialogue is central to Catholic ecumenical work. The pope, in his encyclical *Ut Unum Sint*, describes dialogue as a "common quest for truth in what concerns God and the Church and adherence to the demands of truth" (#18). So it is not simply ecclesiastical negotiation. In the pope's words, in such dialogue there can be "no reduction or suppression of the context of revealed truth, which is to be sought in its entirety" (#18). This is because, the pope says, the unity to be sought "is built on the full context and all the requirements handed down by the apostles" (#78). Without this, full communion will never be possible. At the same time, "in this process one must not impose any burden beyond what is strictly necessary" (*Ibid.*). The goal is necessary and sufficient visible unity.

The bilateral theological dialogues carried on with the major Christian communities start from a recognition of the degree of communion already present, based on baptism and faith in Jesus Christ; and they go on to discuss both common understandings and difficult areas of disagreement. This method, followed assiduously since the end of Vatican II, has produced, nationally and internationally, a large number of agreed statements and reports, most of which still have to be assessed, judged, and received by the partners.

The pope's assessment of this great volume of continuing work, given in 1995, is that it "has been and continues to be full of promise." The pope noted that the various dialogues have dealt with many disputed questions, and he said: "As a result, unexpected possibilities for resolving these questions have come to light, while, at the same time, there has been a realization that certain questions need to be studied more deeply" (#69).

Almost equally as important as these dialogues has been the pope's unremitting round of personal contacts, what has been called his "dialogues of charity." These include the great number of meetings he has had with other Christian leaders as well as with people of all kinds in his pastoral visits all over the world. Some of these visits have been really difficult. This was the case in 1995 in Czechoslovakia, where the pope was due to canonize Father Jan Sarkander, a Catholic priest martyred by the Protestants in Reformation times – but perceived by the Protestants of the country to have persecuted them. The pope's superb human and diplomatic skills were able to reveal the truth about the whole affair; and to turn a situation of conflict into one of new understanding, as he asked forgiveness for the wrongs Catholics had done in the history of the Czech lands, and himself forgave the Protestants for the harm they had done to Catholics.

Then there have been the many visits of Christian leaders to Rome. Some of these were striking, as when, in 1993, the Lutheran bishops of Scandinavia gathered with the pope in St. Peter's to celebrate vespers. Such occasions have been particularly prominent in the case of the Orthodox Churches. Just a year after his election, the pope went to Constantinople to renew personal contacts with the patriarch, a visit which was returned ten years later. Every year a delegation from the patriarch comes to Rome for the Feast of Saints Peter and Paul; and every year a papal delegation goes to Constantinople for the feast of St. Andrew in November. And the pope anxiously awaits the opportunity for more such contacts.

That the stand taken by Vatican II in its Decree on Ecumenism has borne abundant fruit, and has made the ecumenical stance an important dimension in the life of the Catholic Church, is due in very large part to the determined personal efforts of Pope John Paul II; this remains true even if visible unity has not yet been achieved and large questions still remain to be solved.

How is all this to be interpreted? Various responses are given. There are those who say the Church's ecumenical commitment is a sell-out. There are those who interpret that ecumenical commitment, or who practice ecumenism, in a way that weakens the Church's magisterium and reduces the content of the Church's doctrine. Both of these approaches are grievously mistaken; they damage both the Catholic Church and authentic ecumenism. I would like to suggest that the pope's ecumenical teaching and action, and that of the Catholic Church, have to be interpreted in a definite context if they are not to be distorted or to mislead. The context is one the pope himself has unceasingly continued to outline.

In the first place, the context includes the constant concern of the Catholic Church since the age of the apostles for the unity of Christians. To say that the Catholic Church started to be involved in promoting unity only after Vatican II is to be ignorant of the continuing effort of the Church to be faithful to Christ's prayer to the Father that all of his disciples might be one. Vatican II was not the beginning. It was rather a point of major development of the Catholic concern for the visible unity of all Christian communities in the one Church founded by Christ.

For example: after the break between East and West (which came about gradually around the end of the first millennium and the beginning of the second), the Catholic Church never became resigned to the rupture, but constantly tried to heal it. This was the reason for the Council of Lyons in the 13th century and that of Florence in the 15th. Even though they failed to attend, the Orthodox Churches were still invited by the popes to take part in all the subsequent Councils of the Catholic Church. These invitations were never accepted until some Orthodox Churches finally sent observers to Vatican II.

The change brought about by Vatican II was the explicit recognition by the Catholic Church that God did use other churches and communities, despite their limitations, as means of grace, and even of salvation for their members, depending upon what they had kept of the truth and of the gifts originally given by Christ. There was a recognition by Vatican II that there is a real, if limited, communion between those other churches and communities and the Catholic Church.

Secondly, the pope's stance on ecumenism has to be read within the whole living Tradition of the Church. This explains both the new moves the pope has been able to make, and his insistence that what has been given by God cannot be changed or laid aside. The Church herself is a gift of God. The Church has preserved, and hands on in each age with the living voice of its magisterium, the revelation of God in Jesus Christ. The Church communicates in the sacraments, the risen life of Jesus Christ; the saving deeds of Christ, present under the signs of the liturgy, are God's gift to the Church. The Church hands on what she has received, both of revelation and of grace; this is her Tradition, a divinely authoritative Tradition that is the outcome of the abiding presence of the Holy Spirit in the Church.

You cannot do ecumenical work in the Catholic Church without a continual awareness that, despite human weakness and sin, the Church is what the Holy Spirit makes her. It is not ecclesially legitimate to look back to some golden age in the past and use this as the pretext for setting aside dogmas or worship of the Church that may be difficult ecumenically. It is Catholic faith that the Holy Spirit has remained with and has shaped the Catholic Church in the second millennium as in the first. For the Church, Tradition is the continuing presence of the Holy Spirit, and the golden age is now. As the 1989 *German Catechism* says so truly: "The Tradition is Jesus Christ himself as the Lord permanently and effectively present in the Church." It is in the light of this Tradition, and as part of it, that the pope presents his teaching on ecumenism. It is in the light of this Tradition that we have to read and understand that teaching.

So, thirdly, the pope insists that we understand what he is saying about ecumenism in the light of Vatican II. And the Council has to be understood as being in continuity with the great Tradition of the Church. It is a distortion of what the Council taught to suggest that, after the Council, the Church became a different Church from what she was before. The Council was not a great moment of discontinuity, as was the Protestant Reformation. It was one further and highly important step in that living continuity of truth and life which is the Tradition of the Church.

In a highly significant consultation held in Rome in February of this year on the current implementation of Vatican II, the pope stressed the need to preserve the true teaching of the Council by overcoming biased and partial interpretations which have prevented the true newness of the Council's magisterium from being expressed as well as it could have been. He insisted that the only genuine norm for interpreting the Council is to interpret it within the fabric of the whole faith and not outside it, in continuity with the faith of all time. Without simply reiterating Tradition, the Council set out to preserve and enhance it. If we fail to grasp this, we will not understand what the pope is saying and doing about ecumenism.

Fourthly, the pope's ecumenical teaching and action is based on, and has to be interpreted in the light of, the Catholic principles on ecumenism as they are outlined in the Vatican II Decree on Ecumenism, *Unitatis Redintegratio* – just as this Decree, in turn, must be interpreted in the light of Vatican II's Constitution on the Church, *Lumen Gentium*, and the *Ecumenical Directory* of 1993. The first of these principles states the uniqueness of the Catholic Church. I give it to you in the words of *Lumen Gentium* and the Decree on Ecumenism:

> The sole Church of Christ . . . subsists in the Catholic
> Church, which is governed by the successor of Peter
> and by the bishops in communion with him.
> Nevertheless, many elements of sanctification and of
> truth are found outside its visible confines (LG #8).

> . . . The separated Churches and communions . . .
> though we believe they suffer from defects . . . have
> been by no means deprived of significance and impor-
> tance in the mystery of salvation (UR #3).

When it is said that the one Church of Jesus Christ subsists in the Catholic Church, two points are being made,
both of prime importance for Catholic ecumenical work –
and both of which have to be held together. One is a *claim*,
the very large but fully traditional claim that the Catholic
Church is the one unique Church of Christ. The other point
is a *recognition* that there can be something of the Church
found in other churches and communions, depending on
what they have retained of the truth and of the gifts which
Christ gave to his Church in the beginning. The other
Christian churches and communities as such contain something of the Church.

The Catholic Church indeed claims to have the full
truth revealed by Christ as handed on through the apostles
in the Church, as well as the gifts of life and grace
bequeathed by Jesus to his Church; this is to say that the
one and genuine Church founded by Jesus Christ is found
today in the Catholic Church. Only to the Catholic Church
do all the many and wonderful things belong which have
been ordained by God for the credibility of the Christian
faith. At the same time, the Catholic Church recognizes
that, in the words of Vatican II's *Lumen Gentium* quoted
above, "many elements of sanctification and truth are
found outside [the] visible confines" of the Church.

This latter statement, this recognition, has been crucial
for Catholic ecumenical work. In the case of the Orthodox,
it has gone as far as the recognition of them as authentic
Churches. As the pope said in *Ut Unum Sint*: "After a long

period of division and mutual misunderstanding, the Lord is enabling us to discover ourselves as sister Churches once more, despite the obstacles which were once raised between us" (#57).

Such developments with the Churches of the East, and, in a certain but lesser degree with the communities originating in the Reformation, are the fruit of the *recognition* contained in the phrase, "subsists in." They do not, however, diminish the *claims* these words contain, a claim which conditions the recognition. That is why, in 1985, the pope said: "We insist, therefore, that the Catholic Church cannot modify or relativize her teaching or deny the richness of which she, as the communion in which the Church of Christ subsists, is the bearer. But she must be open and sensitive to all the truly Christian endowments from our common heritage which are to be found among our separated brethren" (To the Delegates of Ecumenical Commissions, April, 1985).

In the encyclical *Ut Unum Sint*, the pope readily acknowledges that "many elements of great value which, in the Catholic Church, are part of the fullness of the means of salvation and of the gifts of grace that make up the Church, are also to be found in other Christian communities" (#13). Equally he insists: "The unity willed by God can be attained only by the adherence of all to the content of revealed truth in its entirety" (#18). And, repeating the theme that the one Church of Christ subsists in the Catholic Church, the pope says further: "Full unity will come about only when all share in the fullness of the means of salvation entrusted by Christ to his Church" (#86).

The second of the Catholic principles on ecumenism I also want to look at for a moment; it states that the goal of the ecumenical movement is the unity of Christians in one visible Church; it means unity in one apostolic faith, in one sacramental life, and in one teaching authority and apostolic hierarchy. This is a unity which, despite the divisions among Christians, has not been lost but subsists in the Catholic Church.

The pope describes this as the unity of communion, that is, "the unity which has its divine source in the Trinitarian unity of the Father, the Son, and the Holy Spirit." Communion does not mean, as some Catholics have tried to make out, the unity of human togetherness; it is, says the pope: "None other than the manifestation in Christians of the grace by which God makes them the sharers in his own communion, which is his eternal life"(#9). "Nothing less than the unity of the inner triune of God is the model of the unity of Christ's Church," the pope said to the Delegates of Ecumenical Commissions in April, 1985.

While the deepest roots of this unity are in the divine being, it is a unity in the pattern of the Incarnation of the Son of God; and, therefore, it is a visible unity. It is especially a unity in the profession of the one apostolic faith. That is why the pope in his encyclical identifies five specific areas in need of further study in order to achieve a true consensus with our Christian partners in faith. These areas of further study include Scripture and Tradition, the Eucharist, the ordained ministry, the magisterium of the Church, and the Virgin Mary (cf. UUS #79). There has to be a unity in faith, the pope says, that is maintained by the structures that come from the apostles and are carried on by the bishops in communion with the bishop of Rome.

Unfortunately, the question of the goal of unity continues to be a source of division among Christians. This has been the case since the beginning of the modern ecumenical movement. There are those Christians and communities which, like the Catholic Church, hold that there has to be a unity in faith in one visible Church. Many, however, believe it is more important for Christians to address the problems of humanity together, leaving aside problems of belief. The World Council of Churches, under its present leadership, moves in this direction. Unfortunately, the Archbishop of Canterbury sounded a similar note recently when he said: "Ecological unity may encourage us to move in stages to whatever final form of unity God has in store for us."

Now a brief mention of a third Catholic principle of
ecumenism: it is the place of, and the necessity for, the
papacy. Remarkably, this question concerning the need for
a primate has come more and more to the fore in the main
bilateral dialogues in which the Catholic Church is taking
part; the papacy now figures in current ecumenical dialogue as a great challenge, but also in some ways as a possibility.

The whole question was further thrown into relief by
the audacious proposal which the Holy Father made in *Ut
Unum Sint* (#12) to the effect that he, along with other
Christian pastors and theologians, should look at the exercise of the ministry of the bishop of Rome to see how there
could be, in his words, improvement "in the forms in which
this ministry may accomplish a service of love required by
all concerned." It is necessary, he says, "to find a way of
expressing the primacy which, while in no way renouncing
what is essential to its ministry, is nonetheless open to a
new situation" (#95).

So far representatives of other churches have been slow
to take up the invitation. Some have even been quite negative. And some Catholics with special agendas have seized
upon the proposal, both to minimize the role of the papacy
and to push their tired old programs of "reform." All of this
overlooks the fact that the pope's suggestion can be realis-
tically developed only in the light of his teaching about the
papacy as given in the encyclical. He says: "The Catholic
Church is conscious that she has preserved the ministry of
the apostle Peter, the bishop of Rome, whom God established as her perpetual and visible principle and foundation of unity; and whom the Spirit sustains in order that he
might enable all the others to share in this essential good"
(UUS #88).

The pope makes the point that the power of the papal
office, especially its primacy, lies in the divine intention
inseparable from it as a ministry. It is power for service. The
pope's proposal is that this power, which is of divine gift

and may not be reduced or changed, needs always to be made present and administered in the style of a servant, that is, of a true ministry. It has to show forth as a ministry of mercy born of Christ's own mercy. Without this mercy in its exercise, it would not be an authentic ministry; without the divinely given power and authority, such an office would become illusory for the communion of the Church.

It is a Catholic principle of ecumenism that the office of the bishop of Rome corresponds to the will of Christ. The communion of particular churches with the Church of Rome, and of their bishops with the pope, is, in God's plan, an essential requisite of full and visible communion. It is Catholic teaching that, along with the Eucharist, which is the highest manifestation of communion, the office of Peter is an integrating factor in the communion, which is the unique Church of Jesus Christ. The pope says: "This function of Peter must continue in the Church so that under the sole head, who is Jesus Christ, she may be visibly present in the world as the communion of all his disciples" (UUS #97).

In 1985, at the Extraordinary Synod of Bishops, the presidents of the bishops' conferences of the world highlighted the ecumenical significance of the papacy when they said: "Ecclesial communion with Peter and his successors is not an obstacle but an anticipation and prophetic sign of fuller unity."

All that I have been saying about Catholic principles of ecumenism explains why, in November, 1986, when the Holy Father made a pastoral visit to New Zealand and met with the leaders of other Christian communities in the Catholic cathedral of my diocese of Christchurch, he said: "I am aware that Catholic participation makes new demands on the other churches and ecclesial communities taking part in the ecumenical movement. For we come to it with those Catholic principles on ecumenism formulated in the Decree on Ecumenism of the Second Vatican Council."

Certainly, other Christians do find the claims of the Catholic Church to be an added difficulty in the ecumenical enterprise. What happens in practice, under the impulse of apparently growing ecumenical understanding, is that they often conveniently just forget about them. Recently, the aging Baptist theologian, Harvey Cox, notorious in the 1960s for his book *The Secular City*, said: "Protestants have got used to Roman Catholic claims about some unique status and simply take them with a grain of salt." Even more destructive for serious theological dialogue, though, is when some Catholic ecumenists are tempted to go in a similar direction.

All of this explains why at the present time, when there are real ecumenical achievements, and, at the same time, very considerable ecumenical problems, a crucial part of the ecumenical role of the pope and the Holy See is constantly to recall to Catholic ecumenists, as well as to our other Christian partners in dialogue, the Catholic principles on ecumenism.

This has in fact been done, and has aroused a certain amount of media attention in the last couple of months. The Holy Father has authorized, and has declared to be binding upon Catholics, two documents published by the Congregation for the Doctrine of the Faith: the Declaration *Dominus Iesus* of August, 2000; and the Note on the Expression "Sister Churches" published at the end of June, 2000. Both documents simply take up and apply the Catholic principles on ecumenism as Vatican II stated them. Yet the archbishop of Canterbury is reported as saying that repetition of the claims of the Catholic Church to be unique, which these documents contain, threatens the growing convergence of understanding with Anglicans. Similar things have been said by various Protestant groups and by some Orthodox as well. What, in fact, do these two documents say?

The Declaration *Dominus Iesus* is about the unicity and salvific universality of Jesus Christ and the Church; that is, it refers both to the dialogue with other faiths, asserting the uniqueness of Jesus Christ, and to the ecumenical dialogue with other Christians, asserting the uniqueness of the Catholic Church. It says that there is, in fact, only one Church, the Church of Jesus Christ, which subsists in the Catholic Church governed by the successor of Peter and the bishops in communion.

Then it repeats what is already in the Vatican II Decree on Ecumenism, namely, that the churches which have apostolic succession and a valid Eucharist, but do not accept the papacy, are in close union with the Catholic Church; and they can be true particular Churches, even though they lack full communion with the Catholic Church.

Those communities which have not preserved a valid episcopate and the integral substance of the Eucharist (that is, the churches that stem from the Protestant Reformation) are not Churches in the proper sense of the term. But they are by baptism incorporated into Christ and thus they have a certain though imperfect communion with the Catholic Church.

Both groups, those that are recognized as Churches and those that are not, can share many of the elements of sanctification and truth that belong to Christ's Church; but they derive their efficacy from the fullness of grace and truth entrusted to the Catholic Church. All of this means that the one Church of Jesus Christ does exist, despite the divisions among Christians, and that it is to be found in its fullness in the Catholic Church.

The Note on the Expression "Sister Churches," dating back to the end of June, makes a similar point, but in the light of a specific issue, the question of "sister churches." It says three things.

*One.* The origin and development of the term "sister Churches" is somewhat checkered in its history. It is not found in the New Testament, though there are descriptions of sisterly relations between particular Churches (cf. 2 Jn 13). The term began to be used in the first millennium by the four Patriarchates of the East which were already drawing away from communion with Rome. They claimed to be equal sister Churches along with the Church of Rome, which they would acknowledge as first among equals. They spoke of the four Patriarchates together with Rome as being at the head of the Church. Neither the See of Rome nor any of the popes ever accepted this way of thinking and speaking. The expression was a rejection of the claim of Rome to be Mother and Teacher.

The term came to the fore again in recent times when Patriarch Athenagoras of Constantinople used it in responding to the fraternal gestures and the call to unity addressed to him by Pope John XXIII. From there the term was taken up by Vatican II in its Decree on Ecumenism. A couple of years after the Council, it was used in a formal letter from Pope Paul VI to Patriarch Athenagoras. Finally, Pope John Paul II used the term on several occasions, most notably in the encyclical *Ut Unum Sint*. It should be noted that, when the Decree on Ecumenism, Pope Paul VI, and Pope John Paul II in his encyclical speak of sister Churches, they do so in terms not of the Catholic Church as such in relation to one or another confessional group, but rather in terms of the relation of one particular or local church to another.

*Two.* The Note of the Congregation for the Doctrine of the Faith says that the use of the term "sister Churches" is legitimate when describing the relations between particular churches or groups of particular churches such as Patriarchates or metropolitan provinces. In this sense, it can be used to refer also to the Orthodox Churches. For example, the Orthodox Patriarchate of Moscow and the Metropolitan Province of Milan could be described as sister Churches.

This is the correct and proper use of the term ecumenically. The Note says that, used thus, the term has an accepted sense in the ecumenical dialogue. Cardinal Ratzinger comments: "It is an expression which has become part of the common vocabulary between the Church of Rome and the Orthodox Churches."

*Three.* The Note says further, however, that it is *not* legitimate to use the term "sister Churches" to refer to the one, holy, Catholic, and apostolic universal Church in relation to a local or particular church, for example, in relation to an Orthodox Patriarchate or to all the Orthodox Patriarchates together. The Catholic Church acknowledges each as a true particular Church, even though its communion with the whole Catholic Church is wounded. But it is not correct to speak of any one of them, or all of them, as another Church in which the one Church of Jesus Christ subsists.

The Catholic Church is not the sister, but the *mother*, of any or all the particular Churches. This is not simply a matter of terminology; it is a matter of respecting a basic truth, namely, that there is only a single Church, the one Church of Jesus Christ, which subsists in the Catholic Church. Most importantly, the Note also makes the point that the term "sister Churches" cannot be used for those communities in the West which have not kept a valid episcopate and Eucharist.

The spate of objections in the media to these two recent Roman documents from the Congregation for the Doctrine of the Faith has made clear that while some – the Catholic Church, the Orthodox Churches – understand the term "sister Churches" in an exact theological sense, others see it, in the words of an Anglican ecumenist, "as a friendly thing to call one another, an acceptance of one another that is brotherly or sisterly."

So the pope, through his Congregation for the Doctrine of the Faith, recalls us to the Catholic principles on ecumenism. These principles have made possible great advances in ecumenical relations, but they also give a certain direction to those relations as far as Catholics are concerned. In my opinion, the friction caused by the recent necessary restatement of all this would have been avoided, or at least lessened, had those Catholics engaged in ecumenical work themselves been, and helped their ecumenical partners to be, more alert to these Catholic principles on ecumenism – just as the pope himself has been in his remarkable and fruitful ecumenical leadership.

In an Address to the Roman Curia in 1985, the Holy Father very clearly said: "To give witness to the truth and its demands does not mean putting a brake on the ecumenical movement. On the contrary, it means not letting it rest with facile solutions which do not arrive at anything stable and solid. We must base our re-found unity on a deepening accomplished in common of the faith delivered once for all to the saints; we must discover together all aspects and all the demands of truth; we must accept them and submit to them together."

The Most Reverend J. Basil Meeking, D.D., is the bishop emeritus of Christchurch, New Zealand. He was born in Ashburton, New Zealand, and was consecrated bishop of Christchurch there in 1987. He served as bishop of Christchurch until 1995. In addition, for over twenty years he served as an official of the Pontifical Council for Promoting Christian Unity in Rome. His graduate degrees in theology are from the Gregorian University in Rome. Currently he resides in Beaverton, Oregon, but remains a bishop member of the Pontifical Council for Promoting Christian Unity.

# JOHN PAUL II AND MORAL THEOLOGY

## Rev. Joseph A. Murphy, S. J., S.T.D.

Given the many anthologies of varying quality on *Veritatis Splendor*, it is challenging to offer before this group of scholars yet another commentary on it which would say anything new. Nonetheless, I will attempt a slightly different interpretation of *Veritatis Splendor* because I believe key elements in it yield for us a quite fresh program for the moral life based on Pope John Paul II's wider anthropology.

## I.

I begin with a simple example. A Catholic woman told me recently that she is raising her three sons to be good Christians, to avoid drug use and excessive alcohol, and to follow the Church's teaching on sexuality. To this end she provides different helps for them. They are nineteen, twenty-one, and twenty-three, and they attend the usual parties for their age group. They avoid heavy celebrating and they know better than to drink and drive; however, as a precaution, she insists that they carry in their wallets the phone number of a local taxi service if they should unwittingly consume too much alcohol to drive safely, a plan to which they all adhere and which none of them has yet had to employ.

She then told me that, since they are also successfully committed to virginity before marriage; and since they want to avoid all the consequences of sexual promiscuity which the loss of virginity can offer, she has, in like fashion and with similar reasoning, insisted that, next to the taxi number in the wallet, they also carry at parties a condom in case, against their better judgment, they might be called upon to ward off the results of human weakness arising from sexual indulgence. They have not had to use the condoms yet, either, but they are there just in case.

Something is seriously wrong with this picture, although I cannot spell it out precisely; and although you too can sense that something in this woman's worried reasoning does not fit. In fact, I wonder if it does not require a vision broader than mere casuistry provides to dissect this example adequately and give us a comfortable answer. I can tell you this: there are not a lot of priests, nor possibly even a lot of bishops, who would want to be asked by that lady, "Am I doing the right thing?" They would be tempted to refer her question to a specialist. That is the dilemma we are in. This little practical example is an annoying one because we would prefer to think of morality and theology, and particularly the science of moral theology, in more comfortably abstract and sweeping categories.

Well, I believe that the papal anthropology which undergirds *Veritatis Splendor* provides us an opportunity to see human morality in this desired broader perspective; it also enlightens unsettling cases like the above with which we are so sadly confronted. I would contend in this talk that the moral theology of John Paul II is really at one with his total anthropology, and has to be based upon it, just as morality has to come from dogma and morals from the faith. It is insufficient to begin to derive particular conclusions about the pope's moral theology without studying his analysis of the origins of our human condition.

The first unsettling encounter for those who would begin to read *Veritatis Splendor* is not the challenging talk of intrinsic evil and natural law in Chapter Two; rather, it quickly appears in Chapter One in the confrontation with the rich young man, a story which encompasses the first part of my presentation.

In a sense, the story of the rich young man, who kept the commandments but walked away sad in the face of further moral generosity, holds within itself the comprehensive union of law and freedom as the story of us all. The pope is not offering us a pious scriptural beginning for his moral doctrine, but is confronting us with the spectrum of a graced existence whereby the rich young man stands in that peculiar space between the law and the "more," between the obligation and the ideal. "God alone is good," we hear. Elsewhere we listen to: "Be perfect as your heavenly Father is perfect." That is, keep the law in its great detail, even in the smallest. "I have kept the commandments, Master. What more must I do?"

Actually, the rich man is asking the wrong question. He is asking that which we all ask when we would try to cut the moral life into bits and pieces, to make it a matter of more or less – to make it in a sense a subject of compromise. But the rich young man stands precisely on the border between the person who would do more and the person who would do less; this is because Jesus, in watching him slip away sad, had said to him: ". . . if you would have eternal life, keep the commandments; but if you would be perfect, sell what you have, give to the poor, and, come, follow me."

Why does he go away sad? Perhaps because he doesn't realize that the answer of Jesus displays the inability to rationalize the moral life, to rationalize the human good, and, particularly, the inability to rationalize a life vocation in its uniqueness and in its proper context. Did I have to become a priest? Did Mother Teresa have to become the Mother Teresa we revere? Was she free to do otherwise? The question is slightly unfair and taxes the mind because it offers no satisfying approach to the choice of freedom and of the good. We cannot successfully answer the question of whether Mother Teresa was "obliged" to be the Calcutta nun we admire; or whether it was simply her "option."

On the other hand, one must, as she did, keep the commandments of the law. But must one keep the higher precepts? Can we drive a wedge between the commandments and the precepts if there is a unity within the moral life and within each individual which says that we are either all or nothing in our service of God? The young man went away sad if he was looking for an easy answer and a compromise. But Jesus throws him back to the beginning, before the world was a place of compromise and a fallen den of darkness. Jesus gives the rich young man a hint about human nature and its total integrity: it possessed a gift of freedom that in the beginning was not compromised in any way – just as we cannot accept any compromises, any more or any less, in our understanding of the graced life of the Mother of God.

Although we cannot comprehend any degrees of moral living which would have been there "in the beginning," in the paradise of Genesis 1 and 2, we are, in our fallen world, used to dividing our lives into the merciful judgments of more or less good or evil. The young man in Scripture suffers, however, as do we, precisely from the mystery of a totally uncompromised, totally open and transcendent vocation held in tension against the quantified and practical daily keeping of the law.

What is Jesus's answer to him? It is to keep the law in all of its detail. "Be perfect as your Heavenly Father is perfect," he says elsewhere. In this story of the rich young man we find that the beatitudes and the commandments converge. Hence, he has to go away sad if he cannot accept the total gift. The conclusion of the first section of *Veritatis Splendor* in the pope's many pages effectively tells us that freedom itself is a response to mystery, not to necessity; and that the moral life cannot be rationalized and compartmentalized, but rather in its essence it remains a total claim upon every individual.

Compare this total claim to the total act of self-donation in the final chapter. Because the rich young man returns in the last chapter of *Veritatis Splendor*, he appears, if we would sew the text together, as a companion to the martyrs. Where does a martyr stand? Is he between the obligation and the ideal? The martyr represents the highest vocation in the Church, exalted before the confessors, the bishops, the virgins, the widows, and all of the other saints in the Church's liturgy. At the same time, paradoxically, the martyr seems to be on the verge of sin and condemnation. The alternative to martyrdom is apostasy. The martyr is not allowed to be half a martyr but is only permitted to be one who gives the last full measure. Yet does the martyr appear to be under an obligation, the opposite of which is the ugliest of sins? Fragmentation of the moral life does not fit the life of the saint we are all called to be.

In a sense, a martyr is an eschatological figure who can speak for each of us as a whole and for that which we are all called to in the depth of our being, if we but had our lives put together. It would make no sense for Mother Teresa to be less than what she was. Likewise, it is an odd question to say, "Did I have to marry this person? Do I have to stay in this condition of my vocation? Do I have to be a priest?" These are the things the rich young man was implicitly stirring about in so far as he was trying in some way to enjoy the compartmentalization of his being. If we would all become martyrs, we would be able to sum ourselves up once and for all in such a way that keeping the law of Christ would be a single act, and we would be an integral person who could offer it in a perfect act of self-donation.

That is how Chapter One of *Veritatis Splendor* leads us into the last chapter in such a way as to say: "This is true freedom: the law of Christ, which is uncompromising and total."

## II.

The second chapter of *Veritatis Splendor* contains an exposition of the problems of this total moral self-donation within our current world. You could call it, if you want, the problematic of freedom and nature. Both orthodox and dissident theologians have said, and the Church says it time and again, that the uniqueness of the human condition and of the human individual, its glorification, lies to a certain extent in its freedom. But freedom in our modern age is the kind of reality which celebrates autonomy; it is not merely a rejection of illicit heteronomy, but a total autonomy. Freedom fears that nature will be its undoing, because in a certain rationalistic and in a certain philosophical sense, nature as essence is that which imposes a necessity upon us and, in that way, limits our freedom. In other words, the modern world strays from the truth when it rejoices in its autonomy, if this comes to mean a post-enlightenment exaltation of the self. Modern man then suffers from the dilemma in contemporary terms between history and nature, where history is free and nature is constrictive. This was understood in the Middle Ages as the scholastic conflict between the particular and the universal, a dichotomy which the ancient world reflected as an incompatibility between the one and the many.

In such dichotomies, multiplicity and unity are at odds. Freedom, individuality (the particular), and manyness, instances of change, can stand for fragmentation, decay and evil, in opposition to unity, essence, and eternal, immutable being. If plurality is thus a sign of loss, it would need to be overcome by a reversion in the end to the monadic wholeness of the One of ancient paganism, which would absorb all things into a static unity. If one must reject this form of pantheism, however, and defend plurality, it would be at the expense of unity, because unity would then mean uniformity, absorption, stagnation, and loss of freedom. In favor of plurality, a pre-existing order would need to be overcome to allow for genuine creative freedom.

Translated into our day, these ancient and medieval dilemmas emerge in moral theology when the several advocates of an "autonomous morality" struggle to balance freedom of conscience with given law, be it natural law, scriptural mandate, or even magisterial moral doctrine. An imposed and uniform morality is rejected in favor of a particularized, subjective, and autonomous moral choice.

Those who today would prefer the historical and existential choice of the moral individual over any kind of restrictive command coming from "nature" misunderstand the freedom proclaimed in Chapter One of *Veritatis Splendor*, whether it is the freedom that the commandments give us, or the freedom that the beatitudes and the precepts invite us to follow ever more deeply. But, in the modern world's understanding of it, and also in its understanding of nature, such freedom is compromised. Human nature is acknowledged to be different from animal passivity; and for those people who would dissent from the moral doctrine of the Church, which they regard as stifling, the uniqueness of my nature lies in its simple creativity. If this nature is human and free, they would then argue that "nature is as nature does." That is, unlike the animals, they say, I am not obliged to follow the instincts of nature because I can manipulate and control my environment.

Of course, the absolute manipulation of nature would be suicide itself because suicide would give me absolute control over my being; and would, being atheistic at its heart, deliver me from all imposed moral law – and certainly from any deductions based on a concept of nature which has lost its truth and its freedom. The glorification of the particular choice, ineffable at its core, and inscrutable to outside judgment, exemplifies this rebellion against an oppressive heteronomy.

If the modern moral mind continues to prefer the individual's particular judgment to an imposed moral command, then the denial of universal moral absolutes is not far behind; this is something the pope clearly sees. If a universal moral absolute, something always and everywhere wrong, is a constriction of freedom, then moral judgment is in the end situational. The problem of absolutes in the understanding of freedom and nature is exemplified further when we invoke the scriptural quotation that God alone is good. If God alone is good and is the only real absolute, then there can be no participation in this goodness, and such a God becomes soon remote from the world. An absolute deity will simply recede into the distance and remain unapproachable; and we will never partake of its goodness. If this deity represents essential being itself, eternal nature, then it has even less to do with my freedom.

The point is that modern freedom will endlessly qualify nature and depart from any universal law. Here, I believe, is where Catholic dissent in moral theology has slipped into an autonomous freedom which does not begin, as one might think, with the religious "modesty" of a Reformation heritage. In Reformation ethics, I remain sinful before the absolute who is God alone, and I am weak, fragile and unable to make absolute claims or to employ language like "always and everywhere wrong." The Protestant humility before the divine, which privatizes the situational choice and removes it from the comfort of natural reason and law, is not entirely at one with the mentality of Catholic dissent today. Today's dissent tends to glorify reason over nature and heteronomous law. This is not the Reformation fear of acting like God so much as it is the freedom to say that I am whatever I decide to make myself. Such is my nature and my being, they say – and that is the modern mentality which the Pope himself is battling in *Veritatis Splendor*; it represents the kind of manipulation of the human condition that he must speak against. For example, in-vitro fertilization is the manipulation of the very substance of humanity. Where can one stand to do this?

By way of example, contraception is the manipulation of what has been called, unfortunately, my lower nature. Genetic manipulation is the manipulation of what has become a mere product, the human substance itself. People who dissent from the magisterial teaching on sexuality accuse papal teaching of biologism and physicalism, and, in so doing, succumb to a dualism where the spirit of the independent self exercises over the body that same type of control which it exercises over the sub-personal creation. Of course, even the sub-personal creation is not totally manipulable. We can adjust it sometimes to our advantage (or to our peril), but the point is that the comparison of the human self or the human body to a thing in the world is a misunderstanding of what human nature is and where nature has been found.

This soul-body, or universal-particular, dualism is manifest in the separation of spirit and matter in the following fashion. Consider the phrase, "Always do good and avoid evil." Everyone can agree with this norm; but it is a claim which has no specificity if the absolute, the universal, the spiritual and enduring, or that which is good, remains divorced from a particular embodiment. If the particular good is "scandalous" and effectively unknowable, the concrete singular escapes us. We cannot find where the true good, which is absolute, which perhaps is Divine, ever lands in the world and finds in it any place to rest and to take root. The pope therefore has to deal with this misunderstanding of nature by noting that those who have separated the absolute from any particular moral presence of it must consistently say there is no intrinsically evil act and, consequently, that there are finally no negative moral absolutes.

We come to ask, then, whether anything is always and everywhere wrong. For example, adultery for someone like Richard McCormick is always and everywhere wrong, except that, when he asks what adultery is, it becomes impossible to define because adultery is a tautological term. For him it already contains a description of evil whereby adultery is already by definition illicit sex, and illicit sex is, of course, always illicit. "Adultery" adds no objective information to "Don't have illicit sex"; it is really a subset of "Don't do anything wrong." McCormick would say the same of torture and a number of other things that many of us would call intrinsically evil, holding as he would that our intrinsic evil language is unable to catch, unable to land, unable to define evil – because the evil in them is already absorbed into a prior definition. As general rules they give us no practical information.

In searching for agreement on an intrinsically evil act, William May reports in one of his footnotes asking McCormick the question about the immorality of sex with an animal. He received no answer, presumably because there could be circumstances, exceptions no doubt, where, since animals are good and sex is good, sex with an animal does not implicitly contain anything wrong in itself apart from the circumstances. I would take exception if McCormick said this, and say, as I suppose many of you would say, that we can make statements about intrinsic good and evil. Sex with a nine-year-old is always and everywhere wrong for anybody in this room, at any time, willing or unwilling, as the participants may define it. If so, this would mean that there is some truth which is utterable about the world, some understanding of the world that actually contains the possibility of good and rejects the possibility of evil.

But the battle the pope has on his hands is with this rejection of intrinsic good and evil, using the excuse that the particular case is unrelatable to evident participation in the universal good. The particular must then have reference finally to itself, for its rightness or wrongness; this is a position which seriously compromises the meaning of objective morality. I once heard Charles Curran say, for example, that the Church can easily proclaim its doctrine in matters of dogma, but in morality and in practical matters, things are always changing and are not so clearly definable. This is an ancient opinion, as when the material singular, the concrete act or person or thing, is unintelligible in itself. This conclusion is actually similar to a Reformation mentality which would say, pretty much like the Protestant principle which Paul Tillich championed, that human reality, all things under heaven, cannot bear the Divine (the eternally universal), except perhaps distantly in an eschatological fashion in faith, in expectation of a holiness that they cannot have here because no human institution or earthly item can in a fallen world call itself intrinsically good or intrinsically holy.

The contemporary doctrine which this Reformation view translates to morally, for the pope, is that of proportionalism, which means that, if everything is negotiable, the concrete good really resides nowhere – because until all of the conditions are known, we cannot fix the good anywhere except in our conscience and in our judgment. The conscience which the pope explains in *Veritatis Splendor*, however, is not a law unto itself, is not merely a subjective intention, but is actually much more. It is a response, a response to a law in our members and a law in our being.

The pope faces also the same problem of this calculus of the proportionate good when he describes the shortcomings of the fundamental option theorists. He notes how the fundamental option is frequently misunderstood or abused, much like the general command to go about doing good and avoiding evil gets lost in abstraction, as we pointed out above. "Be just, be whole, be moral." But some proponents of fundamental option seem to say that no particular act can express my wholeness sufficiently; and that nothing I do can sum me up adequately in the way, for example, that the martyr at his death participates in total self donation – the same donation asked of the rich young man when invited to the full acceptance of his vocation. Moreover, they deny that the particular act can be sufficiently meaningful to express my underlying nature and being; this again is a position the pope thoroughly rejects.

What then do we do with these interpretations of Christian behavior in our world today, where the pope is really exposing the limitations of contemporary morality in its misunderstanding of nature, its denial of particular intrinsic goodness and evil, and its denial of moral absolutes? We must answer how anything under heaven can be absolutely good. Not infinitely good, but absolutely good. How can anything here and now be real and lasting and have value? To understand this I think I have to turn beyond *Veritatis Splendor* to those things that are repeated in it but more implicitly.

## III.

Throughout his document the pope keeps referring to the time "in the beginning." "In the beginning it was not so," says Jesus, when he is talking about celibacy for the disciples. The pope reminds us about the "beginning" because in the beginning there was a different order. In the beginning there did not exist the solitary self of the creature Adam exercising his autonomy. The pope announces in *Veritatis Splendor* that freedom, while it is not totally heteronomous, is certainly not autonomous; it is theonomous; and there is no such thing in Genesis for Adam or for us as self-definition. This is what it means to be made in the image of God. It is to have one's experience of self, of being-in-the-world, as totally referential, as from, for, and with, not as an enclosed ego.

The question, then, is whether being made in the image of God is an oppressive consignment, or a liberation? That there is no self-definition or self-creating in Genesis is evidenced by the dialogue about the tree of paradise: "Do not touch this tree." If we cannot eat that fruit, there is something said about us which we do not control, which we do not create. The tree is the moment of truth, of good and evil. It is my awareness of dependence, something I have not given myself. As Joyce Little remarks so well about Genesis, Adam names the animals, not himself. He can name them and claim them as their master, whom they serve because he is in the image of the creator who has ultimate dominion. But Adam is not ultimately self-naming, just as the man described in *Veritatis Splendor,* when the pope exhibits his scriptural interpretation of freedom, is also one who is not self-defined, but one who is created in the image and likeness of God, and one who is given and gift by his nature.

It is remarkable what the pope does with Genesis 1 and 2 because of his understanding of "person," especially compared to commentaries where an older interpretation or traditional interpretation of the image of God prevails. When most of us first studied theology and philosophy, imaging God was explained as being spirit, as we noted above, in having intelligence and will, even being like the angels who, some say, image God more perfectly than we do in their nearness to the Divine. Is it too bad that we are not angelic or pure spirit? Is it the case that we would be better off if we were? This older interpretation, or, I should say, this quite accurate and traditional one which the pope also quotes in *Veritatis Splendor* refers to the image of God as spirit. If that is the case, the body which "carries" this image and relates man to the sub-personal creation is prone to the misunderstanding of having a dualist relationship to this spirit. The "newer" understanding of the image of God – and I call it new only because the pope has found new ways of describing it – is really based on Genesis 1:26–28, where the text reveals that we are created male and female and in the image of God. These verses produce a radical transformation of the understanding of the image of God, and a radical transformation of the self, because they express the marital or the nuptial foundation of reality. In other words, to be human is not merely to be an individual, a human thing, a free nature, an isolated thinking and acting self, but it is to participate in a substance and in a union with someone else or with others in a reality that transcends the individual. To be a totally autonomous individual is to be, in the sense Genesis forbids, self-creative. "They would be as gods" means that they would decry God and would be whoever they wanted to be themselves.

Some of this understanding has crept over through philosophy into the classic Boethian definition of person as a substance of a rational nature, a human individual. If we go back, however, to Genesis 1 and 2, we find that the solitary self, the individual man, which the pope describes in his interpretation of original solitude, and which he distinguishes as alone by being apart from the animals, is further alone until he is in relation with another person. There is no man, not as male, until there is a woman. There is no woman until there is man, and there is no real humanity until the human species exists and it is the human species as marital, nuptial or covenantal, which becomes the foundation of the moral life. It becomes the foundation of the moral life because it is there where the person becomes truly personal – by being not alone but interpersonal. In this understanding, the body does not have to be adjusted to the spirit – as if spirit were the imaging of God, and the body a point of negotiation within the created world: as if man were a unique mixture of angel and beast. Rather, the imaging of God includes the body as well, since the body is the expression of the spirit. Rather than man being individually the image of God, male and female in the image of God constitute in their union a tri-relational reality. Man, woman, and their bond image by analogy the Trinity itself, which is the prime analogate here.

We tend to think, as taught by Boethius, of each individual as a separate substance to which co-personhood or interpersonal being is an accidental relation. In the Trinity we understand substance and relation (person) rather differently. Cardinal Ratzinger has pointed out that, through the Trinitarian doctrine, relation has come into its own on a par with substance. The pope's theology of the body leads us to rediscover the notion of substance and relation on the human level as analogous to the divine. Norris Clarke has said that to be a person is not merely to be a substance of a rational nature, but it is to be substance in relation. Perhaps the pope would say that to be a person is to be substance through relation, to be and to exist in and through another, in much the same way that Jesus describes Himself as having nothing of His own but as being transparent to the Father. Put negatively, another way of saying this is to consider the radical understanding of sin as a refusal to be, not just a refusal to do this or that. The virtue which is then the opposite of any sin is a particular acceptance of my being in and through another with God as last end, as we say, and not so much a mere doing of some good external act.

Self-acceptance then becomes understood not as an

introspective psychological achievement of personal ego-identity, but as an acceptance of relatedness to God. Concretely, it means living and having my being in the Body of Christ. The body of Christ is in a special sense the true substance. It is better called, perhaps, not substance but a union, a term greater than our ordinary conception of substance. Unlike the static substance of traditional philosophy, the Body of Christ is a free substance, one that I must join in order to exist truly. I will say, then, that for the pope Christ is the formal cause of reality, but I say it in such a way that I must belong to Christ by freedom. He is a formal cause unimposed and free, but with the radical intimacy which form has to matter.

This leads us again to say that the human species is by nature radically covenantal. The conclusion of the pope's anthropology is therefore that sexuality is primary and total, a doctrine he holds throughout his writings about the unity of human sexuality. As such sexuality is anything but accidental. William May has spoken of being male and female as entitative habits and I think that is quite accurate. Sexuality is constitutive of the human species; it is not something which can be transcended and, consequently, it is not something I own but something that precedes me and something which owns me. I do not think it is possible, therefore, in defending the dignity of the body, and in holding to the doctrine of intrinsically evil actions, to avoid sexuality as the most immediate, available place where we find intrinsic goodness.

Why is the Church so preoccupied with sexuality, her critics ask? Because therein lies the basis of our being and the substantial location of all subsequent moral interaction. You cannot, for example, show that there is anything wrong with in-vitro fertilization if the human individual is understood as only a quantity. In that case, sexuality is seen to be nothing but a function. If it is a function it can produce goods; but if there is another way of producing the goods, there is nothing wrong with utilizing the new way by producing the in-vitro baby. But if the pope is right, and we are fundamentally not personal in an isolated sense of our solitude, but are always co-personal, then it is the case that this co-personhood which the human individual enjoys is part of his very identity.

In other words, to be human is to be received. To come into this world is not to be produced as a product or objectified as a human unit; but it is to be sexually loved into the world as part of one's very identity, as something which cannot be forgotten and replaced. Otherwise, if sexuality is not thus self-defining and the covenant not dominant, there can be no reason in the world against further manipulation of the male/female relationship – such as gay marriages, contraception, sterilization, and, particularly, the test tube baby. Why is this baby not a positive gain, and the more human babies the better? If they are common goods and usable goods, then the more we have of them, the more personal the world is.

But the papal anthropology holds that it is an indignity to be a product-baby because to be is to be received and to be given, given not merely by will and desire but also to be bodily given and bodily loved into existence sexually. It is for this reason that the dignity of the human person and of the body is unable to be separated from our sexuality so as to become a useful and functional thing unto itself. If Adam and Eve are not self-defining but received, so in marriage – or in whatever way we image the covenant – we too are received in our being; here, precisely, is the locus of the intrinsic good.

When we search for things that are intrinsically evil, we find that such evil cannot exist except by further reference. We have to find it as a variation on that which is intrinsically good. What the Church is teaching, according to the pope, is that the human condition is given as holy as a mystery of our faith, a truth not sufficiently otherwise available through philosophical reason or through some analysis of the natural law. It is given with the first act of faith, and it is given as an existential intuition, as Paul discovers in Ephesians, when he describes the salvific act of Christ in marital terminology. He makes the case that the human substance or the human unit, or whatever you want to call us – humanity itself – exists in this covenantal relationship and is given its identity as something that we cannot manipulate.

Derivatively we can then say that the Church's teachings on sexuality will be the first place where intrinsic good and evil is found and reflected. Subsequently, lesser created things will not be so intrinsically good and evil except in reference to the human. Property, for example, can be negotiable, such that it is not material cooperation for me to give my wallet to a thief at gunpoint. It is, however, a degree of formal cooperation for the woman in the concentration camp, in the famous case often cited, who sleeps with the guard to obtain her freedom. In that situation, we have a different kind of "property" and a quite different degree of (non)-negotiability at stake.

What's the difference? The difference is the nearness of the person, the nearness of the whole understanding of the self, the place where good created reality finally encounters its identity and finds its primacy: in human sexuality and in the nuptial meaning of the body. It is this intrinsic good and its correlative intrinsic evil which really proclaims our morality as concrete and returns us to our beginning.

Now we can finally ask where the true beginning is. Jesus refers to our beginning where we will truly find human nature. If we could divine what our nature is, it seems we could lock on to what we truly are, and we would confront our morality within it. Human nature for the pope throughout his writings and, certainly, in *Veritatis Splendor*, with its references to the beginning, is already in Christ. Moreover, it is in the covenantal Christ, not simply in the new Adam, but in the relation between the new Adam and the new Eve. The Incarnation, in other words, is not simply a doctrine about the two natures in one person of Jesus, as much as it is a doctrine of the Christ-Event, the union of Christ and his Mother, the New Covenant. This foundation of reality continues for us in the relation between Christ and His Church and, therefore, Christ is called the bridegroom of the bridal Church. It is a foundation reflected in the marriage of every man and woman who imitate and re-enact that relation between Christ and the Church in their sacramental and historical existence; it is a relation, the violation of which through adultery makes evil to be concrete.

We really have to say, then, that the pope in *Veritatis Splendor* departs from the philosophical conundrums engendered by an over-application of a natural law reasoning too dependent on philosophy, or resulting from the stifling debates over freedom and nature. He turns instead to Revelation, and sees the order of creation and the order of grace as one. It is difficult to establish a moral theology simply laid on top of a natural ethics if all of the good in the universe is the good of Christ, just as all grace is the grace of Christ. The beginning where we are most immediately defined is in Christ (and in Mary), and therefore he is able to be our true law.

This covenantal relationship reflected in the union between Christ and the Church, and reflected in every sacramental marriage, is continued in the Eucharist as the ongoing Christ event whereby liturgical actuation is that which makes the world to be a world. The text of Ephesians 5 gives us that unique understanding of the moral life as it is related to the Eucharistic life and to the covenant itself in its marital structure.

All of those other interpretations of sexuality as functional or partial or manipulable reassert themselves if we depart from this radical understanding. Submit sexuality to a ratio and very soon most variations are justifiable – once it is subject to my reason alone. But if my sexuality is a received condition, pre-reflectively, and deep within my consciousness and my basic self-awareness as interpersonal, I cannot objectify it sufficiently nor submit it to extensive analysis. The reception of it is not a matter of simply being burdened with sexual urges or with fixed bodily rhythms. It is rather to be given an integrity, a fertility, and a generativity which is structured around marriage and the covenantal relations we exemplify when we call people mother or father or sister or brother and identify them as members of a covenantal relationship within the Body of Christ.

As for the freedom we spoke of earlier, it is most aptly defined as a response to mystery, a condition most genuinely ascertained in the relation between husband and wife. What about the negative moral absolutes which John Paul II defends? They are defined negatively because they direct us away from sinful limitations of fragmented fixation upon a creature and direct us toward the human good as mystery. They can thus be universal, whereas the positive moral absolute, the personal calling to a particular human good, can vary by vocation. Everyone can agree that the rich young man must avoid thievery and fornication, but no one can oblige him to do what only he knows the Lord is uniquely calling him to. He must avoid all directly chosen evil, but he cannot do all the possible good in the world.

Where the negative moral absolute cuts us off from the idolatry of things, the positive moral absolutes, which we know largely as the beatitudes, are, though not necessarily properly, "optional" callings, which are unique and personal. Freedom, therefore, is not endless optionality, or some freedom of indifference, but is the freedom to embrace the good without restriction; to embrace my nature as it is given to me in freedom and mystery and not by imposition.

We could ask again whether there is a natural law that competes with freedom. The covenant provides a solution. When people get married, for example, they freely do so. It is not a choice which can be imposed, nor is it a condition that can be simply deduced from general principles. It is a free response to an offer of love not experienced as binding "law." Once married, however, the spouses join a reality bigger than themselves, an objective order, a reality which they cannot dismiss without dismissing part of themselves. They participate in a radical nature, if you want, but a nature which at every moment remains mysterious and free. That is the result of understanding them as free in their very essence, but as relational and not as self-determining in every respect.

Christian existentialists like Marcel have used expressions, as if in anticipation of the pope's anthropology, expressions such as, "I am my body" – as if to avoid a residual dualism between spirit and matter. But if the body is also the locus of personhood – that is, if male and female differ as persons precisely because of their sexual configuration – then we find in the pope's doctrine the understanding of the self as fundamentally co-personal. If I indeed am my body, then I am essentially interpersonal, not accidentally so.

This co-personhood is primordial in Genesis in its anticipation of the original covenant which, in our world, is grounded historically and metaphysically in the free incarnational union between Jesus and his mother; this is the place where our true nature manifests itself. For John Paul II, then, nature is not best understood as a prior natural order lying under a supernatural order. It is not even simply an order of reason enriched by faith. It is rather that world which has fallen and is redeemed and now in sign possesses the Eucharistic Lord until he comes again. For the pope all history is salvation history. In the beginning God did not make a linear cosmos or a calendar of material occurrences. In the beginning there is Christ and his Mother, at least in the ontological or the metaphysical sense, and as that covenantal pair which orders the world to follow them through the Incarnation, while looking back before it to a fallen world in anticipation of it. The intrinsic good and evil which we look for in actions are found in the intrinsic goodness of the free man and the free woman of Genesis – or of the Christ and Mary of human history. In the end we return to that co-personal integrity from which we are fallen, and we do so by our attachment to the holiness of the body, Christ's Body initially, which empowers us to live by holy deeds in an integral world.

I return to the point with which I began. What can I tell that Catholic lady with three sons? I can say something about the kind of person my actions make me and I can counsel her not to live in such fear. The Catholic tradition, against recent dissent, has reasserted through the words of the pope the mystery of true personal freedom. I cannot be a proportionalist because every embodied act defines me and describes the type of person that I would become. I thought of this lady who wants to give her son something to take in his wallet when Janet Smith raised this morning the issue of using condoms in preventing AIDS. We sense that there is something wrong with that suggestion and with its inherent capitulation to the defeatist claim that "they're going to do it anyway." One of my colleagues, in 1987, when the bishops were ready to endorse condoms, cleverly asked why they didn't just encourage masturbation as a lesser evil. Should the mother with her three sons perhaps so encourage them?

Let me use another example. Some nuns in Africa who were threatened with rape in the 1960s were given permission to use a kind of birth control pill. That is a moral position not without difficulty, but the actual defense of it was based to a certain extent on the principle of a proximate attack and, therefore, it was a case of double effect through self-defense. It does not easily translate to an application to the AIDS question. I do not wish to go into the particular cases, but I do wish to derive from what I have said so far that the kind of person we are underneath everything else is the person speaking and uttering the truth about us.

I will extend the above example. Suppose that we agree that these nuns in Africa could use the pill to maintain their integrity. Now, suppose a young woman, a law student, imagines she will be married by age thirty, but now at age twenty-three she is staring at several years of singleness. Now suppose as well that there existed a perfect form of safe temporary sterilization which was 100 percent reversible. Can she sterilize herself against the prospect of her own folly, fully intending to be chaste, fully intending to observe the moral law, and successfully doing it now, but "just in case"? What does that do to her? Is fertility simply a tool to be used and invoked later on, or, rather, in the intervening seven years, is she not also a fertile and a life-giving person? The only way I can begin to answer her or the mother is to refer to the self-definition of the person as fundamentally sexual and therefore to the reality of sexuality as an all-encompassing primary identifying fact about each of us; and it is a fact which is non-negotiable.

I would say no: you cannot undergo a sterilization against the possibility of your folly, even if you intend to remain chaste all of those years. What are you saying about yourself and your dealings with the world? The lady in the concentration camp story actually did sleep with the guard, went free, and returned to her family. What are the goods that come from that? Proportionally, they seem worthwhile. In fact, a child was born of that union. At home she can raise her daughters to get a good education, so that they one day get married; and if there is a war, and if they end up in a camp, and in turn sleep with the guards to save their daughters – who down the line would do the same thing, then – what are we saying here? Where in this world does God's created law, the law which frees us, truly take root? Where is the non-negotiable side of the human person which may not be compromised?

The pope has answered this again and again in his location of basic human reality in its sexual configuration, and in the definition of the human species as marital and nuptial. It is that kind of reality with which we are dealing. If God alone is the source of good, and if we as creatures have received of that goodness, we can image and participate in it and its primacy. We can participate in the covenant which is that of the Lord Jesus reflected in Christ and the Church, reflected again in each marriage, and which goes back to the very beginning. God alone is holy, but he makes us holy if we keep His will and if we follow His law.

Father Joseph A. Murphy, S. J., is a priest of the Missouri Province of the Society of Jesus. He is currently the academic dean for both the College of Liberal Arts and the School of Theology at the Pontifical College Josephinum in Columbus, Ohio, where he has also been Associate Professor of Moral and Sacramental Theology for the past two years.

He has lectured frequently the on life issues and published previously on the topics of abortion and the civil law. His previous contribution in the area of the above talk was: "Human Solidarity in the Ecclesiology of John Paul II," prepared for the Jesuit bi-annual symposium on the work of the pope.

# JOHN PAUL II AND
# CHRISTIAN PHILOSOPHY

## Ralph McInerny

When you are scheduled last on a program, you don't know whether you are meant to be dessert or bromo-seltzer. But perhaps this placement is due to the fact that I am a philosopher in his twilight years, and am best heard in this twilit hour. One of course remembers Dr. Johnson's friend who had thought of becoming a philosopher, but cheerfulness kept breaking through.

We do stand at an odd juncture in the history of philosophy, and Cornelio Fabro's judgment seems to be borne out. Speaking of the subjective turn taken by Descartes, Fabro wrote: *sic incipit traegedia hominis moderni;* here begins the tragedy of modern man. The seeds of atheism were present in methodic doubt, and, once sown, they have now grown with their deadly fruit. No wonder that in *Gaudium et Spes*, the Fathers of Vatican II gave us a little treatise on atheism in their effort to sketch the profile of the contemporary who is the object of evangelization. The pathology of modern philosophy is one of the leit-motifs of Pope John Paul II's *Fides et Ratio*.

Those Catholic philosophers who welcomed the appearance of *Fides et Ratio* just two years ago, in September, 1998, are not among those the American philosophical establishment tends to tout. Describing the average anything is an exercise in imagination, of course, but providing a profile of the typical professional philosopher in this country would not be difficult. Call him Quidam. Hearing that the pope has issued a book-length letter on philosophy, Quidam's first reaction would be nonexistent. He couldn't care less. But if prodded to notice, his wry smile would prepare you for his words. "Either by 'philosophy' the pope means the teaching of his Church, or he means the sort of thing I do. If the former, perhaps what he has to say is of interest to his co-religionists, and that is fair enough – as long as they don't try to impose these views on others. But if he means the latter, his remarks are simply irrelevant. Philosophy cannot be guided by the religious beliefs – if any – of its practitioners, let alone by letters emanating from the Vatican."

Quidam might be interested to learn that the encyclical speaks of him and that his views play a role in its unfolding drama.

## 1. The Stances of Philosophy

In Chapter VI of *Fides et Ratio,* we find a number of paragraphs (#75–78) gathered under the heading *"Different stances of philosophy."* These are distinguished historically, although their instantiations need not be confined to any historical period. The pope speaks of *(a) philosophy completely independent of the Gospel's Revelation;* (b) *Christian philosophy; and (c) philosophy as autonomous and self-sufficient.*

While later thinkers might compare what Plato and Aristotle had to say, for example about God, with what God has revealed about himself, such a comparison was not possible for Plato or Aristotle. They simply pursued inquiry using such light as is available to the human mind, and their results would be assessed with reference to the validity of argument, the truth of premises, and so forth. Some early converts who had had the benefit of an education in Greek philosophy thought that it was completely superseded by Revelation, and could be left to history or to any surviving pagans. This was far from being the majority view, however, and many such converts developed various sophisticated versions of the relationship between what the philosophers taught and the truths revealed by God in Christ.

It is this second attitude that gave rise to the second stance that *Fides et Ratio* mentions – philosophy as carried on by Christians. Quidam, who holds the autonomous and self-sufficient view of philosophy, a view that, as often as not, sees a natural enmity between philosophy and Christian beliefs, is, of course, opposed to the idea that anything like *real* philosophy could take place under Christian auspices. Real philosophy is something totally other than religious belief and ignores it, either because it occurred prior to any acquaintance with Christian faith, or because the philosopher has discarded the Christian belief he had or schizophrenically resists any temptation to bring the two into relationship with one another.

## 2. The Autonomy of Philosophy

It is important to see the strength of Quidam's position. By anyone's account, philosophical discourse is characterized as setting off from starting points which are in the public domain, that is, accessible to anyone with standard cognitive equipment. No philosophical argument can depend upon premises which are not in principle knowable by any human without reference to religious belief. Quidam, in reminding us of this, might invoke Thomas Aquinas to support his point. The problem with Christian philosophy, Quidam would say, is that it seems to be what Thomas means by theology – which, of course, Thomas opposes to philosophy. The mark of theological discourse is that it is intrinsically dependent on revealed truths, which are held to be such on the basis of faith, and not because they are seen or known to be true. But philosophical discourse is not at all like that. No truths of faith are to be found among its premises.

In short, philosophical discourse is one thing; theological discourse is another and different thing, and there seems to be no *tertium quid* possible. But Christian Philosophy is precisely such a putative *tertium quid*, an illegitimate hybrid. *Ergo, et cetera...*

One need only go back to the debate between Mandonnet and Gilson at the famous Juvisy meeting of French Thomists in 1933 – that had as its topic Christian Philosophy – in order to find Thomists who argue as Quidam does, invoking as I imagine him doing, the authority of St. Thomas Aquinas. Mandonnet counters any defense of Christian Philosophy by repeating that Scripture, Revelation, truths held on the basis of divine faith, *cannot* function in philosophical arguments.

His opponents repeat the equally solid truth, the historical truth, that within the ambience of Christianity, philosophy developed in ways it otherwise would not have, that the influence of the faith is seen in the emergence of certain concepts, in the direction of certain arguments, and so on.

The two sides spoke past one another for much of the day. That philosophy as it developed in the ages of faith bears the stamp of that influence is undeniable. That truths of faith cannot be the hinge on which philosophical arguments turn is equally undeniable. The latter truth can lead to schizophrenia, with the believer ignoring what he believes as he pursues the truth, and thus, for all practical purposes, adopting the autonomous and self-sufficient view dear to Quidam and his cohorts. The former truth – the undeniable influence on philosophy during the ages of faith – can lead, and, in the case of Gilson, did lead, to an effective denial of any important difference between Thomas's philosophy and his theology.

## 3. Y-a-t-il une Philosophie Chrétienne?

The dispute of seventy years ago had been prompted by a tendentious article of Emile Bréhier which questioned whether anything that could truly be called philosophy had gone on in the Middle Ages. Will Durant, Betrand Russell, and other lesser figures, told the story of philosophy in such a way that it leapt over the thousand years of the Middle Ages because nothing "we" would call philosophy had been going on during those benighted centuries.

The thought of Bertrand Russell poring over medieval folios in search of a philosophical argument and coming up empty stretches one's credulity, of course. The view was a priori; it was not the result of any serious study of medieval thought. But the same could not be said of Bréhier, who deserved, and received, responses from those who thought otherwise. Looking back on those times, it seems that every French Catholic thinker produced a book with the title *La philosophie chrétienne*. Bréhier's question had clearly struck a nerve, and the believing philosopher felt compelled to achieve clarity on the matter. And, as the Juvisy conference showed, there were sharp differences, even between Thomists, as to the correct way to state the relations between faith and reason, faith and philosophizing.

In the light of this, we can imagine Quidam's reaction if he should read that Christian philosophy "seeks rather to indicate a Christian way of philosophizing, a philosophical speculation conceived in dynamic union with faith" (#76). This will sound like the dynamic union of oil and water, of black and white, of up and down. And Quidam's mood will not alter as he continues.

It [Christian philosophy] does not therefore refer simply to a philosophy developed by Christian philosophers who have striven in their research not to contradict the faith. The term Christian philosophy includes those important developments of philosophical thinking which would not have happened without the direct or indirect contribution of Christian faith (#76).

Quidam's worst fears are now realized, and he feels confirmed in his conviction that whatever thinking is consequent on religious belief or the influence of the faith will simply not be philosophical. Call it philosophy if you like, but it cannot be "real philosophy."

## 4. In Quest of Real Philosophy

Quidam will wax eloquent if you ask him what real philosophy is. He has contrasted it with what he regards as its bogus twin, Christian philosophy. Why bogus? Because the believing philosopher does not enter upon the philosophical task with clean hands. Meaning, empty hands. He comes to the table with convictions and beliefs which guide and hem in his inquiry, and which prevent him from following the argument wherever it goes. He is prejudiced. He has a closed mind.

From such accusations, the conception of real philosophy and real philosophers begins to emerge. Unlike his Christian counterpart, the real philosopher, e.g., Quidam, is uninfluenced by any beliefs he might have outside the seminar room. Settling to the philosophical task, his mind is a *tabula rasa*. Quidam is not given to seeking support in the history of philosophy, but it would occur to him to say in this connection that it is the defining mark of Modern Philosophy – Modern Philosophy being the resumption of real philosophy after the millennium that separated it from pagan antiquity – the defining mark is to subject to methodic doubt all the contents of the mind; to set aside or put in escrow whatever furnishings the mind might have picked up along the way to beginning to philosophize.

Such systematic voiding of the mind of alleged knowledge, doubting it away, paved the way for an absolute starting point, a first step which met the criteria of clarity and certainty. Then a step-wise progression could begin that remained immune to any outside influences. A lot has happened to philosophy since Descartes, but Quidam is inclined to think that the essential thing has remained, namely, that philosophizing cannot start from or be guided by beliefs, prejudices, or outside influences. It is autonomous and sufficient unto itself.

Kierkegaard began an account of a student attempting to follow the injunction that philosophy finds its beginning by means of doubt – he called it *Johannes Climacus or De omnibus dubitandum est*. The point of the unfinished story is that the presupposition of modern philosophy, universal doubt, is impossible, so either philosophy itself is impossible or universal doubt is not its presupposition. Quidam will not have read Kiekegaard, of course, and would be

disdainful of the suggestion that anything written in the
1840s might disturb his notion of what real philosophy is.
But Kierkegaard's point is of permanent relevance.

Quidam, now a paunchy fellow in his late fifties, began
life as a child. He had parents and was raised by them. He
acquired a view of the world from his home, his neighborhood, and eventually from his schools. And then one day
he went off to Meatball Tech where he signed up for
Philosophy 101 because the girl ahead of him in line had
just done so. Her name was Fifi LaRue. Fifi's rapt attention
in class was mimicked by Quidam, but soon his interest
was no longer feigned. By sheer chance he had enrolled in
a class taught by the renowned Gottfried Hamburger.
Hamburger, of course, was a refugee from Vienna, and he
had brought to the New World the beliefs his circle had
been describing in that storied city. In short, Quidam was
introduced to philosophy in its guise as Logical
Empiricism. Later, supine on the campus sward, he would
read A. J. Ayer's *Language, Truth and Logic* aloud to Fifi, and
its iconoclastic insouciance drew them closer together. But
it was over the pages of Hans Reichenbach's *The Rise of
Scientific Philosophy* that they kissed for the first time.

Let us draw the veil over such intimacies. What have
we learned thus far? One, that Quidam began the study of
philosophy by accident. Two, that he happened to gain a
notion of what philosophy is from a renowned member of
the Vienna Circle. Third, Quidam was disposed to find
books that expressed the viewpoint of Logical Empiricism
congenial, indeed, almost aphrodisiacal. As he waxed in
years and study, his philosophical bent became more pro-
nounced. He and Fifi no longer spoke much to one another, but when they did it was in the accents of the revered
Professor Hamburger. So now the question: What would it
mean to say that Quidam comes to the philosophical table
with clean, that is, empty, hands?

Our acquaintance with some aspects of his history will
not dispose us to think of him as Pure Reason, without
antecedents, beliefs, hands and feet, and a tendency to

quarrel with Fifi. Why is all this supposed to be irrelevant yet the believer's faith disqualifying? Quidam will reply that none of that matters when he is doing philosophy. Once at the table, his mind is purged of prejudice, antecedent beliefs – the lot. He is at epistemological Square One. But then what will the topic of discussion be? Where will it come from? Quidam brought it with him, of course, or someone else in the room did; and the question put will be understood in terms of previous questions discussed; and possible answers to it will occur to Quidam that might not occur to his colleague Aliqua, a fetching phenomenologist with reference to whom Fifi has developed a jealous streak.

As Unamuno put it, philosophers are creatures of flesh and blood, not pure minds. *The ideal of 'real philosophizing' is an impossibility for a flesh and blood human being.*

## 5. What Has Been Gained?

The point of showing that anyone, Quidam included, brings to his philosophizing a rich personal history, antecedent beliefs, dispositions, hunches, and hopes, which influence and guide him as he chooses a problem and goes in quest of its solution, is clear. How could it be otherwise? Thus, a first response to Quidam's characterization of the believing thinker's situation is, *Et tu, Quidam? Tu quoque, amice!*

But a moment or two spent savoring this triumph is followed by unease. What has been gained may seem the reduction of philosophy to ideology. Is all this search for arguments and truth really guided only by a desire to support the prejudices with which one began? If so, since we begin from different antecedent convictions, the result seems to be a terminal diversity of results. We have hopelessly relativized philosophical positions. Each of them can be parsed back into the antecedent beliefs and dispositions of the thinker. How then could any be true save to one who happened to share those antecedent beliefs? Christian philosophers will thus seem to be thinkers whose antecedent beliefs coincide. Quidam and those who attend his favorite satellite session at the APA are similarly bound together not by arguments, but by the prejudices out of which the arguments come.

How might Quidam, and the Christian Philosopher, dispute this outcome? Each would now agree that they have antecedent beliefs. But like Quidam, the Christian Philosopher will contend that the arguments he puts forward are meant to persuade anyone who follows them. However much they grew out of his antecedent beliefs, each philosopher would say that you need not share his beliefs in order to see the cogency of his argument. There is little prospect that this liminal agreement, if reached, will be the dawn of concord and unanimity. As I have revealed, even Quidam and Fifi quarrel. What counts as cogency? What will be accepted as an appropriate philosophical method?

Well, there is no need to continue the list. Agreeing on the terms of agreement is no mean feat. Still, something has been gained in persuading Quidam that he is a man of flesh and blood, *pace* Fifi. We may leave him in the hope that he will be less inclined to read other philosophers out of court on the basis of a fantastic self-misunderstanding.

## 6. Christian Philosophy

But can the Christian philosopher rest content with this equation of his condition with that of Quidam's? Will he be attracted by the suggestion that his faith is an antecedent condition that will be surmounted in the course of philosophizing and thereby drop out of sight? That faith is a first stage of the rocket which drops away as he soars on into transcendence? Surely he will find this to be a churlish attitude toward the gift of faith.

John Paul II distinguishes two aspects of Christian Philosophy, one subjective, the other objective. By the objective, he means the believed truths that might suggest or become philosophical projects. I believe that God is free and personal. Could I establish that in such a way that a non-believer would see its truth. As Gilson once suggested, the program of Christian philosophy is made up of the *praeambula fidei* – those truths which, though de facto revealed and accepted on faith, are in themselves knowable and can be established on a basis other than faith. The richness of the believer's resources here are incalculable, and he will be disinclined to see them as on a par with the baggage that Quidam brings to the philosophical table. Far from seeing himself on an equal footing with the secular philosopher, the Christian philosopher will cherish the enormous advantage of a storehouse of truths vouchsafed by God's revelation, accepted on faith, but also productive of philosophical research projects that would never occur to the secular philosopher.

The subjective aspect of Christian philosophy has to do with the moral virtues which attend the philosophical life. The importance of character in grasping the truth in moral matters is obvious. As Newman put it, good and bad men judge differently. Since philosophizing is a moral task, it will be facilitated or impeded by the moral condition of the thinker. This is dispositive. But the pope suggests something further, which seems to link the subjective with the objective aspect of Christian philosophy. "The philosopher who learns humility will also find courage to tackle questions which are difficult to resolve if the data of Revelation are ignored – for example, the problem of evil and suffering, the personal nature of God, and the question of the meaning of life or, more directly, the radical metaphysical question, 'Why is there something rather than nothing?'" (#76).

## 7. The Defense of Reason

*Fides et Ratio* reminds us of the many ways in which the faith, far from being an obstacle to philosophy, is an enormous aid to it. And in these dark days, perhaps the greatest service faith does is to come to the defense of reason itself. The relativism we touched on above, as the possible upshot of taking into account the existential condition of one who philosophizes, was something we were concerned to show did not follow from the argument. And our assumption was that Quidam, as well as the believing philosopher, would be concerned to defeat this charge of relativism. Well, Quidam has fallen in with strange philosophical companions in these days. There is a fashionable Nietzschean nihilism abroad in influential philosophical circles that accepts – though, of course, it cannot state – the view that truth in any robust sense is a concept that has had its day. The assumption of philosophers, friends and foes alike, has always been that the claims they put forward were true, that is, were underwritten by the nature of the things they were talking about.

That is the assumption that is no longer made by many. Philosophical claims are no longer taken to be verifable in that way. There is no reality to which they might correspond. If the term truth survives, it is merely to cover success in persuading others to adopt your assertions. They cannot, of course, be persuaded by any appeal to objective support for what you say. There is none. You must win them with rhetoric. But why? As an instance of the will to power, apparently.

Against this background – and who can say how deep it has penetrated into the contemporary philosophical mind? – the defense of the range of reason and its capacity for truth in *Fides et Ratio* takes on new importance. No believer can accept the relativist and nihilist standpoint. His faith presupposes and thus shores up his confidence in our capacity to know.

One might regard this as a minor benefit of *Fides et Ratio*. Perhaps. But in an age that has lost confidence in the capacity of reason itself, the believer must be reminded that his faith as well as his experience underwrites the view once shared by philosophical opponents – namely, that one of them was right and the other wrong. The Principle of Contradiction may not look like the epistemological equivalent of climbing Mount Everest. But from the beginning of philosophy's long history, the greatest philosophers have spent great amounts of time protecting the life of reason from the encroachments of skepticism and sophistry. Error is a bad thing but incoherence is worse. One of the surprising boons of Christian Philosophy, consequently, is that it is a charter of sorts for error and falsehood. Where they are impossible, truth is equally impossible. Of course, truth is better.

The awful impasse in which we now find ourselves has been described by John Paul II as the battle between the Culture of Life and the Culture of Death. This latter day opposition is the ultimate fruit of the change of starting points at the outset of modern philosophy. Methodic doubt is based on the assumption that ordinary folk do not really know anything; apart from the ministrations of philosophical doubt they can never responsibly say they *know*. Nonsense, of course. Ordinary folk know many things without any help from philosophy. Properly understood, philosophy takes its rise from those commonly known truths. Among them are fundamental moral truths, the precepts of natural law.

But the obvious has become obscure in the Culture of Death. A good part of the philosophical task in our own day is to recover the obvious. Kierkegaard said that the reason we have forgotten what it is to be a Christian is that we have forgotten what it is to be a man. In his *Letter to Families*, John Paul II reverses this. The reason we have forgotten what it is to be human, is that we have forgotten what it is to be a Christian. Both men are right in their different ways.

The specifically philosophical mode is argument, and the irrationality of the presuppositions of the Culture of Death must be exposed. But there are ideas which, like devils, are driven out only by prayer and fasting. This is a message that Mary has been bringing to the modern world in a series of apparitions. And, of course, *Fides et Ratio*, like just about everything else John Paul II writes, ends with remarks about the Blessed Virgin. Christian philosophers have long understood that their motto must be: *philosophandum in fide: philosophize in the ambience of the faith.* John Paul II recalls an early monastic Marian devotion and provides us with a motto we might paste up over our desks. *Philosophari cum Maria: philosophize in company with Mary.*

Ralph McInerny, Michael P. Grace Professor of Medieval Studies and Director of the Jacques Maritain Center at the University of Notre Dame, took his Ph.D. at Laval University in Quebec, and is the author of many scholarly works, including *The Logic of Analogy* (1961), *Thomism in an Age of Renewal* (1966), *Aquinas on Human Action* (1992), *The Question of Christian Ethics* (1993), and *Aquinas Against the Averroists* (1993).

He is also a novelist and author of the Father Dowling, Andrew Broom, and Notre Dame series of mysteries, including, most recently, *Irish Tenure* (1999), *The Book of Kills* (2000), and *Heirs and Parents* (2000). Recent non-fiction works of his include *What Went Wrong with Vatican II ?* (1998) and *The Defamation of Pius XII* (2000). Professor McInerny has been the recipient of various fellowships (Fulbright, NEH, NEA) and is a fellow of the Pontifical Academy of St. Thomas Aquinas. He is a past president of the American Metaphysical Society and the American Catholic Philosophical Association as well as of the Fellowship of Catholic Scholars (and a recipient of the latter's Cardinal Wright Award).

For many years editor of *The New Scholasticism*, he is also the founder and publisher of *Catholic Dossier*; and, with Michael Novak, he was a co-founder of *Crisis: A Journal of Lay Catholic Opinion.* Under his general editorship, the Jacques Maritain Center at Notre Dame has launched a twenty-volume edition of *The Works of Jacques Maritain.* He is also publishing a six-volume edition of *Aquinas's Commentaries on Aristotle.* He delivered the Gifford Lectures at the University of Glasgow in 1999–2000 (to be published in book form by the University of Notre Dame press).

# CARDINAL WRIGHT AWARD BANQUET REMARKS

## Mary Ann Glendon

I am deeply grateful for this honor, especially when I contemplate the names of the persons who have received the Cardinal Wright Award in the past. I feel very fortunate indeed to be in the company of so many people who have been an inspiration to me in so many ways.

A few weeks ago, Professor Bradley mentioned to me that the remarks made by previous recipients of this award have centered around a common theme – the experiences of "the faithful Catholic intellectual in today's academic world." So I took his comment as permission to contribute my own two cents on that topic.

I can think of no better capsule description of the role of the Catholic intellectual in the academic world than that chosen as the theme of this conference: Witness to Truth. George Weigel brought out the same thing in his magnificent biography of Pope John Paul II: *Witness to Hope*. The hallmark of Catholic scholarship is that it is oriented towards both hope and truth – borne along, as the Holy Father says, on the wings of faith and reason.

There was a time, of course, when almost any academic, Catholic or not, would have insisted that his or her scholarship was oriented toward truth. That was a time, as some of us remember, when it was also taken for granted that we would strive for objectivity in our research. Certainly those were the elements of the credo of my mentors at the University of Chicago. And that must have been the idea behind the choice of "Veritas" for the motto of

Harvard University as well. In fact, the original Harvard seal had the words "*Christo et Ecclesiae*," ("for Christ and the Church"), around its border. Veritas was in the center along with three books. Two of these books were open, symbolizing revelation in the Old and New Testaments, and the third book was shown closed, signifying that not everything is accessible to human reason.

Modernity and the Enlightenment changed all that. First, Christ and the Church were eliminated; then, the third book was shown open! Veritas, however, remained.

But a funny thing happened to Veritas in the secular universities on their way to *post*-modernity. It became harder and harder to find many intellectuals *other* than Catholics who were willing to affirm the existence of truth, or the once-prized values of reason and objectivity. Perhaps the next edition of the Harvard seal will place Veritas in quotation marks to reflect the triumph of relativism in the secular academic world.

So where does that leave the Catholic intellectual? I would argue that it puts him or her in the vanguard. The fact that our forebears were never totally swept up by modernity has, I believe, helped us to harvest the benefits of modernity while avoiding many of its pitfalls. It helped us to avoid the kind of hubris about truth that has led so many heirs of the moderns first into disappointment and then into cynicism and nihilism. Catholic scholars seldom flatter themselves that they are in complete possession of the truth. We have always understood that human beings in this life apprehend truth only as through a glass darkly. But that does not mean that truth does not exist, nor that we cannot draw closer to it through our God-given capacity for reasoning in the light of faith.

It helps us, too, that Catholic intellectuals never bought into the Hobbesian notion of reason as calculation in the service of self-interest. Our tradition understands reason in terms of the recurrent, collaborative, and potentially self-correcting processes of human knowing – experiencing, understanding, and judging. Catholic intellectuals thus tend to value qualities that seem to be in increasingly short supply in the post-modern academy – qualities such as freedom of inquiry, willingness to listen to those who do not share our views; and also respect for the accumulated wisdom of those who have gone before us.

So far as objectivity is concerned, a lively understanding of sin preserved us from the illusion that we can ever wholly rise above our biases and blind spots. But we also know that we must not ever stop striving to overcome those failings. As Clifford Geertz memorably put it, the fact that a surgeon can never have a completely sterile operating field does not mean he has to conduct surgery in a sewer. In this struggle, too, we are sustained by our great intellectual tradition.

Rarely a day goes by when I do not thank God for that tradition. And I am sure that all of us members of this Fellowship feel the same. How fortunate we are to be Catholic Scholars! Yet here is a puzzle: recently I had a queasy feeling when I saw myself described in a law review article as "the Catholic scholar Mary Ann Glendon." It was an article on the legal profession and the author had cited many writers besides me. But he did not refer to the others as the Jewish scholar X, the Marxist scholar Y, the knee-jerk liberal scholar Z. I was the only one given a special identifier. I wear the label "Catholic" as a badge of honor, of course, yet I can't help wondering whether the label here was in the nature of a warning to the reader: this author, unlike the rest of us, has a bias; she alone may not be a disinterested seeker of truth.

It was a trivial incident, but it reminded me of what my favorite law professor, the emigre scholar Max Rheinstein, told me about the German academy in the 1930s. One of the first signs that the great German universities were becoming corrupt was that Rheinstein (a Christian of Jewish descent) and others, when cited, were labeled as Jewish authors. Later, it was forbidden to cite them at all. I am not suggesting, of course, that any of us is in danger of being rounded up or driven into exile. But I imagine most of us here have had little experiences of exile – when our work is not mentioned in the literature dealing with subjects on which we have written, when our books are not reviewed, or when our writing is handed over for evaluation to persons who do not give us a fair hearing.

Am I suggesting that the intellectual establishment in this tolerant and politically correct age is anti-Catholic? Not at all. The knowledge class loves Catholics – at least a certain kind of Catholic. Peter Steinfels explained the situation well in a recent *New York Times* column. He reported hearing a woman with a reputation for supporting "liberal" and "humanitarian" causes discussing her son's wife at a Washington dinner party. After singing the praises of her daughter-in-law, the woman said, "She's a Catholic, you know, but she's a thinking Catholic." Steinfels surmises that what the woman meant was that her daughter-in-law is a Catholic who dissents from the Church's teaching wherever it conflicts with reigning moral and political dogmas. If you're a "thinking Catholic" in that sense, the welcome mat is laid out for you. You can help the reigning elites to maintain that they are not anti-Catholic.

If, on the other hand, you're just a "Catholic Scholar," you'd better look for fellowship somewhere else. And what a fellowship we have! What companions, living and dead! And what a joy it is to be in each other's company this evening!

Thank you all so very much.

Mary Ann Glendon is the Learned Hand Professor at the Harvard Law School. She holds several degrees, including that of *Juris Doctor* from the University of Chicago. Prior to joining the Harvard law faculty in 1986, she taught at the Boston College Law School and worked at the private practice of law in one of the nation's most prestigious law firms.

Mary Ann Glendon is one of the leading Catholic academic women in the world. She is an internationally recognized authority in the fields of comparative law and family law. Her book, *Abortion and Divorce in Western Law*, is a classic in its field. Her other books include *Rights Talk* and *A Nation Under Lawyers;* and she recently completed a book on human rights and international law, *Rights From Wrongs.* She is also the author of the recent and acclaimed study, *A World Made New: Eleanor Roosevelt and the Universal Declaration of Human Rights.*

Professor Glendon was the first woman to head a Vatican delegation to an international conference, the U.N. Conference on women in Beijing, China. She is also a founding member of University Faculty for Life.

# FELLOWSHIP OF CATHOLIC SCHOLARS

Membership Information
http://www4.DESALES.edu/-philtheo/FCS/

## Statement of Purpose

We, Catholic Scholars in various disciplines, join in fellowship in order to serve Jesus Christ better, by helping one another in our work and by putting our abilities more fully at the service of the Catholic faith.

We wish to form a Fellowship of Catholic Scholars who see their intellectual work as expressing the service they owe to God. To Him we give thanks for our Catholic faith and for every opportunity He gives us to serve that faith.

We wish to form a Fellowship of Catholic Scholars open to the work of the Holy Spirit within the Church. Thus we wholeheartedly accept and support the renewal of the Church of Christ undertaken by Pope John XXIII, shaped by Vatican Council II, and carried on by succeeding popes.

We accept as the rule of our life and thought the entire faith of the Catholic Church. This we see not merely in solemn definitions but in the ordinary teaching of the pope and the bishops in union with him, and also embodied in those modes of worship and ways of Christian life, of the present as of the past, which have been in harmony with the teaching of St. Peter's successors in the See of Rome.

To contribute to this sacred work, our Fellowship will strive to:

Come to know and welcome all who share our purpose;

Make known to one another our various competencies and interests;

Share our abilities with one another unstintingly in our efforts directed to our common purpose;

Cooperate in clarifying the challenges which must be met;

Help one another to evaluate critically the variety of responses which are proposed to these challenges;

Communicate our suggestions and evaluations to members of the Church who might find them helpful;

Respond to requests to help the Church in her task of guarding the faith as inviolable and defending it with fidelity;

Help one another to work through, in scholarly and prayerful fashion and without public dissent, any problem which may arise from magisterial teaching.

With the grace of God for which we pray, we hope to assist the whole Church to understand her own identity more clearly, to proclaim the joyous gospel of Jesus more confidently, and to carry out its redemptive mission to all humankind more effectively.

To apply for membership, contact:
Rev. Thomas F. Dailey, O.S.F.S.
FCS Executive Secretary
DeSales University
2755 Station Avenue
Center Valley, PA 18034-9568
TEL: (610) 282-1100, Ext. 1464
E-mail: THOMAS.DAILY@DESALES.EDU

*Fellowship of Catholic Scholars Quarterly* – All members receive four issues annually. This approximately 50-page publication includes:
President's Page
Scholarly articles

Important Documentation
Bulletin Board (news)
Book Reviews
Occasional Fellowship symposia
*National Conventions* – All members are invited to attend this annual gathering, held in various cities where, by custom, the local ordinary greets and typically celebrates Mass for the members of the Fellowship. The typical convention program includes:
Daily Mass
Keynote Address
At least six scholarly Sessions
Banquet and Awards
Membership business meeting and occasional substantive meetings on subjects of current interest to the Fellowship's membership
Current members receive a copy of the published *Proceedings* containing the texts of the speeches of each national convention, with other material of interest sometimes included.
*National Awards* – The Fellowship grants the following awards, usually presented during the annual convention.
*The Cardinal Wright Award* – given *annually* to a Catholic adjudged to have done an outstanding service for the Church in the tradition of the late Cardinal John J. Wright, Bishop of Pittsburgh and later Prefect of the Congregation for the Clergy in Rome. The recipients of this Award have been:
1979 – Rev. Msgr. George A. Kelly
1980 – Dr. William E. May
1981 – Dr. James Hitchcock
1982 – Dr. Germain Grisez
1983 – Rev. John Connery, S.J.
1984 – Rev. John A. Hardon, S.J.
1985 – Dr. Herbert Ratner
1986 – Dr. Joseph P. Scottino
1987 – Rev. Joseph Farraher, S.J., & Rev. Joseph Fessio, S.J.

1988 – Rev. John Harvey, O.S.F.S.
1989 – Dr. John Finnis
1990 – Rev. Ronald Lawler, O.F.M. Cap.
1991 – Rev. Francis Canavan, S.J.
1992 – Rev. Donald J. Keefe, S.J.
1993 – Dr. Janet E. Smith
1994 – Dr. Jude P. Dougherty
1995 – Rev. Msgr. William B. Smith
1996 – Dr. Ralph McInerny
1997 – Rev. James V. Schall, S.J.
1998 – Rev. Msgr. Michael J. Wrenn & Mr. Kenneth D.
        Whitehead
1999 – Dr. Robert P. George
2000 – Dr. Mary Ann Glendon

*The Cardinal O'Boyle Award* – This award is given *occasionally* to individuals who actions demonstrate a courage and witness in favor of the Catholic faith similar to that exhibited by the late Cardinal Patrick A. O'Boyle, Archbishop of Washington, in the face of the pressures of our contemporary society which tend to undermine the faith. The recipients of this award have been:

1988 – Rev. John C. Ford, S.J.
1991 – Mother Angelica, P.C.P.A., EWTN
1995 – John and Sheila Kippley, Couple to Couple
        League
1997 – Rep. Henry J. Hyde (R.-IL)